THE TERRY LECTURES
The Religion and Science Debate

The Religion and Science Debate
Why Does It Continue?

Edited by
HAROLD W. ATTRIDGE

With an Introduction by
KEITH THOMSON

Essays by
RONALD L. NUMBERS
KENNETH R. MILLER
ALVIN PLANTINGA
LAWRENCE M. KRAUSS
ROBERT WUTHNOW

Yale University Press   *New Haven & London*

Published with assistance from the foundation established in the memory
of Philip Hamilton McMillan of the Class of 1894, Yale College.

Designed by James J. Johnson and set in Stemple Garamond types by
Keystone Typesetting, Inc. Printed in the United States of America.

Library of Congress Cataloging-in-Publication Data

The religion and science debate : why does it continue? /
edited by Harold W. Attridge ; with an introduction by Keith Thomson ;
essays by Ronald L. Numbers ... [et al.].
p. cm. — (The Dwight Harrington Terry Foundation lectures on religion
in the light of science and philosophy)
Includes bibliographical references and index.
ISBN 978-0-300-15298-2 (cloth : alk. paper)
ISBN 978-0-300-15299-9 (pbk. : alk. paper)
1. Religion and science. I. Attridge, Harold W. II. Numbers, Ronald L.
BL241.R35 2009
261.5′5—dc22
2009010792

A catalogue record for this book is available from the British Library.

This paper meets the requirements of ANSI/NISO Z39.48-1992
(Permanence of Paper).

10 9 8 7 6 5 4 3 2 1

Contents

Preface

Over the course of a century the benefaction of Dwight Harrington Terry in 1905 has brought to Yale an array of distinguished scientists, scholars, and theologians who have reflected in various ways on the relationship between scientific exploration and religious faith. Lecturers normally grace Yale's campus for a period of time, ranging from a week to a semester, and give a series of lectures usually published as a book. The occasion of the centennial celebration of this significant lectureship inspired a different format. In the face of ongoing controversy in the United States about the relationship between science and religion, particularly evolutionary biology and traditional readings of the biblical creation story, the Terry Committee decided to focus on that debate and to ask why it continues with such force. The Committee invited a panel consisting of two scientists, a philosopher, a historian, and a sociologist, asking them to reflect on the debate from the vantage point of their disciplines. The lectures for 2006 thus consisted of a lively interchange among distinguished scholars and scientists and active dialogue with an audience of Yale faculty and students. This collection of essays is the result of the efforts of our lecturers, refined by their interactions with one another and with the Yale community. The introduction by distinguished scientist Keith Thomson ably sets the stage for the individual contributions.

The task of turning the presentations into published form involved the efforts of several colleagues. Members of the Terry Committee, Leo Hickey, Bill Summers, Dale Martin, and Michael Della Rocca, commented on the essays and made suggestions for their improvement. Joyce Ippolito did a splendid job of copyediting the final products. Jean Thomson Black of Yale University Press coordinated the editing efforts and facilitated contact with the authors. Lauralee Field provided unwavering staff support for the Committee and kept the whole process moving efficiently.

The Terry Committee hopes that the essays collected here serve as more than a historical snapshot of a particular moment in American culture, also helping to clarify what has been and is at stake in the sometimes tense intersection between two vital spheres of human endeavor.

HAROLD W. ATTRIDGE

Introduction
The Religion and Science Debate:
Why Does It Continue?

KEITH THOMSON

"Epicurus has set us free from superstitious terrors and delivered us out of captivity . . . while we worship with reverence the
transcendent majesty of nature."

CICERO, *de Natura Deorum*

S cience and religion, science versus religion: the subject was argued by the ancient Greeks and scholars of the Middle Ages and the Enlightenment.
In choosing this subject for its centennial occasion, the
Committee for the Terry Lectures has highlighted an issue that is both ancient and modern, exquisitely complex and painfully simple. The one certainty that we share
with our intellectual forebears in this matter is the need
for well-considered dialogue. For both Cicero and David
Hume (*Dialogues Concerning Natural Religion*) a dialogue was not just a literary device but the best way to discuss "any question of philosophy . . . which is so obscure
and uncertain, that human reason can reach no fixed determination with regard to it: if it should be treated at all,

seems to lead us naturally unto the style of dialogue and conversation. Reasonable men may be allowed to differ, where no one can reasonably be positive."[1]

The mission of the Terry Lectures is to discuss "religion and its application to human welfare in the light of scientific knowledge and philosophical insights." The intensity of the modern "debate" seems to leave little room for considering the wider issue of human welfare, but in fact all five authors of the following essays agree that the debate has serious social consequences in terms of education and a broader public discussion of science and society. Robert Wuthnow approaches the subject from the viewpoint of a sociologist, Lawrence Krauss as a physical scientist, Kenneth Miller as a biologist, Ronald Numbers as a historian, and Alvin Plantinga as a philosopher. While the basic issue concerns all of science, the bellwether point of contention is evolution.

There is bound to be a debate because science and religion are two very different entities with different ways of arriving at "truth." Both have claims on both our reason and our intuition. They have a long history of difficult relations. Sometimes they are compatible; sometimes they are at odds. But, while traditionally religion has felt under threat from science, now science is more equally under threat from religion as well. As Kenneth Miller says in his essay here, "The perception of scientific hostility to religion . . . lies at the very root of the antievolution movement in the United States," and, as Wuthnow says, "in the United States at least, religion is perhaps the only cultural institution with reasons to confront science that also has the resources to pose criticisms."

There are many questions. Is intelligent design (and its

underpinning creationism) religion? Is evolution good science? Is science competent to adjudicate among supernatural issues? Is religious belief ever a reason to ignore or suppress good science? What are the limits to the explanations that evolution can provide for questions of natural and supernatural phenomena? How should religion be dealt with in schools (and elsewhere)?

The eminent scholar John Hedley Brooke reminded me long ago that there are many different kinds of science and of religion.[2] Before one can make the categorical statement that "creationism" is a religious construct, or that the hypothesis of intelligent design is not science, definitions need to be established. (This being the United States, the courts have been called upon to do this for us and have recently gone a long way to resolving these problems. But that does not mean that hearts and minds have been changed.)

On religion, Wuthnow writes here that "popular assertions about religion typically assume that it is readily defined by belief in God or resort in some way to arguments about the supernatural. Yet scholars of religion seldom define it in those terms. . . . [Geertz defines it] as a system of 'symbols, powerful and long-lasting motivations, and conceptions of a general order of existence clothed in an aura of factuality.' " He goes on to point out that this revised definition can be thought to apply to science.

The core debate, of course, is not concerned with such niceties. Looked at in the context of this debate, Geertz's definition is perhaps necessary, but definitely not sufficient. The debate concerns first and foremost the "popular assertions"—that there is a God who controls our lives

and destiny and who is worthy of worship. Fundamental
mental and moral attitudes result from this belief, as well
as standards for a spiritual and practical life. In all religions there is an element of particular rites and ob-
servances, and many symbols. (The critical reader will
identify my use of extracts from the definition of religion in the old *Oxford English Dictionary*.) The average
school board member, anguishing over what he or she has
been told about evolution and about intelligent design,
probably neither knows nor cares about definitions like
Geertz's (which, in any case, sociologists and philosophers continue to wrangle over). That person would
positively bristle at the use of the phrase "*resort to* . . . the
supernatural.*" He or she would also be well aware of the
recent attacks on religion by scientists such as Richard
Dawkins that have contributed nothing but rancor to the
debate and removed it yet further from being a dialogue.

None of our authors quite defines science, which the
same dictionary defines in terms of a method of enquiry,
applied to organized knowledge, leading to the discovery
of general laws, and restricted to those branches of study
that relate to the phenomena of the material universe
and their laws. Several authors do refer to the scientific method, which has a proven track record dating back
at least to Francis Bacon and which has been embellished
by modern philosophers of science, particularly by Karl
Popper's criterion of falsifiability. One must also acknowledge boldly that science is not equipped to deal
with situations where observations cannot be made directly, measurements taken, or experiments performed.
It therefore resists or rejects the world of miracles and
the supernatural, demanding of it the same proofs as ap-

ply in the material world. If, one day, the sun actually were to be observed to move ten degrees backwards (II Kings 20:11), Copernicus, Galileo, and every cosmologist after them would have been wrong. In contrast, modern psychological and genetic science has ventured into the search for material explanations of religious behavior.

There are, of course, many slippages between the ideal in science and religion and the realized product. Science suffers in the public eye because it does not always find a single unalterable truth. One of the reasons the space shuttle can land in the right place is that the gravitational constant is not a matter of political opinion, technological fashion, or religious edict. But scientific knowledge in many other areas is a moveable feast. Perhaps science's greatest liability when it comes to public understanding and acceptance is that it proceeds by making a changing and progressively more uncommon sense out of common sense, and the new versions are always far more complex and arcane-seeming than the original (Einstein's physics versus Newton's, for example). People distrust a science that gives changing, more refined, answers. We dislike being told that, having learned something, we must then try to relearn it, especially if that is very difficult. We also tend to resist conclusions that the sky is falling.

Despite this complexity, or rather because of it, science —however defined and however practiced—has revolutionized our world, particularly in the last 150 years. Few would now wish to live in a world without satellite communication, smallpox vaccination, anesthesia, or more prosaically, processes of refining hydrocarbons.

Whatever benefits there may be to a religious individual

in terms of the conduct of one's life on earth and promises of a life to come, all religions set high moral and ethical standards for society in both "spiritual and practical life," and these have formed the basis for whole civilizations. In our own case, to isolate the precise role of Christianity in Western history would be impossible; it is also impossible to deny that its role has been immense. Often this has been for good but sometimes not, and (as with science) where different versions of religions have come to be associated with political movements, great evil has been accomplished in their names. However, neither in science nor in religion would we, nor should we, condemn the greater whole for lapses in the execution of parts.

Religions may have an advantage over science because they are seen as founded upon a number of immutable truths. But this can be a disadvantage if, fairly or unfairly, they are seen as imposing a body of truths that must be accepted on faith and revelation rather than discovery and analysis. And we have to acknowledge that, as Wuthnow explains, "neither science nor religion can be quite as easily compartmentalized into separate and noncompeting domains." At times science seems to act like a religion: it has its high priests, its truths, symbols, and shibboleths, its body of received wisdom, and its sects. It claims to encourage dissent while sometimes actually suppressing it. No one gets burned at the stake, but careers can be made or ruined. What makes science fundamentally different from other kinds of human endeavor is the self-policing method of enquiry at its core.

If some of the above seems like a caricature, my aim is to emphasize that what matters in the *public* debate is not what philosophers and historians write but the simplified, and sometimes simply wrong, version that the general populace "knows." There is a continuing debate, not because of esoteric philosophical discussion in the groves of academe where, as here, mutual respect is required and conciliation is to be sought, but because of the hopes and fears expressed in pulpits and school board meetings across the country. The debate continues not just because science and religion are both immensely powerful, in the sense of having a history of changing the lives of billions. It is because they are perceived to be based on entirely different principles that are relentlessly leading us in different (potentially opposing) cultural directions. It has to do with the ways, and the extent, to which humans have the power to control and shape their own world. And with who gets to exercise those powers. Because power is involved—institutional power and individual empowerment—inevitably so is fear. And fears can be exploited by the unscrupulous.[3]

All this has relatively little to do with evolution, per se; the differences are more fundamental and concern science as a whole. If Charles Darwin had not given mechanistic teeth to the ancient question of transmutation of species, science would still be at odds with religion. The acrimony of the debate would perhaps be more focused on other subjects like the Big Bang singularity and the material basis of the mind and soul where, as the White Queen said, we cheerfully believe "six impossible things before breakfast." The debate would exist as it does now, and it would be just as multifaceted. Post-Enlightenment philosophers would still have wanted to free thought from the perceived straitjacket of religious and other dogma.

Some scientists would still use science, as did Thomas Henry Huxley and John Tyndall (see Numbers's essay) as a tool to promote the secularization of society, and as the antidote to one based, in their minds, upon "superstition" rather than fact.

Without Darwin, geologists would still have discovered a number of key facts about the history of the earth, particularly that the fossil record incontrovertibly demonstrates a sequence of changes in life on earth over a period of more than two billion years. These are facts that require us to change—to accommodate—our world view. Plantinga, in his essay here, dismisses them as "a *proposition* that the earth is billions of years old and a 'progress *thesis*'" (emphasis added). That the earth is extremely old is a fact. It is one of those uncommon truths of which our understanding has changed over the past two centuries— in Darwin's time the age was estimated at a million years or younger. It is possible to *believe* that the earth is only a few thousand years old, but impossible to *know* that. Similarly, the sequential integrity of the fossil record cannot be dismissed as a thesis. It is a fact, and a falsifiable fact (what constitutes "progress" in the record is a separate question). Every day and every hour, someone somewhere is testing that fact by digging somewhere new, or digging again in the old places. If a human fossil were ever demonstrably found in the arms of a Triassic dinosaur, or a mammal tooth embedded in a Silurian trilobite, the equivalent of the sun moving backward through the skies would have occurred.

What Darwin added to the study of transmutation was, as was obvious to him at the time, extremely dangerous. He demonstrated both a result—divergent change—and a mechanism—natural selection. Modern science then documented and amplified them. Organisms are not just related to each other genetically, they are related through genealogy—this is testable and provable through studies of DNA. If we trace back the demonstrable history of life on earth, we all have ancestors in common, hierarchically —as humans, as mammals, as vertebrates, as chordates, as animals, and as organisms in the first place. "Evolution" is both the pattern of these changes over time and the name we give to the process by which they occurred.

The science of evolution does not require any external supernatural cause to account for its changes. Even more dangerously, evolutionary theory predicts that the very first living organisms arose out of nonliving organic precursors through the operation of the same natural laws and processes (like variation and selection) that caused the subsequent divergences. It invokes no supernatural guidance in initial "creation." We must note well that this is a prediction, whereas the subsequent evolution of life on earth is fact. Evolutionary science does not claim to know *as a fact* that the first living organism self-assembled out of nonliving material. Every decade seems to bring us a little closer to a view of a possible mechanism, and then the answer slips away again. Science also does not have any evidence either for or against the occurrence of anything supernatural after that initial creation. This is precisely where, as Hume said, "no one can reasonably be positive."

The single most dangerous thing about evolution, however, is that it has the power potentially to explain away the greatest mystery after the origin of the universe itself. It is the quintessential example of the oft-repeated statement of Stephen Weinberg: "Science does not make in impossible to believe in God. It just makes it possible not to believe in God."

There is no use in appealing to Charles Darwin on this issue. The very last sentences of his 1844 manuscript outline for his eventual *On the Origin of Species* show him arguing against the theological approach: "From death, famine, and the struggle for existence, we see that the most exalted end which we are capable of conceiving, namely, the creation of the higher animals, has directly proceeded. Doubtless, our first impression is to disbelieve that any secondary law could produce infinitely numerous organic beings, each characterized by the most exquisite workmanship and widely extended adaptations: it at first accords better with our faculties to suppose that each required the fiat of a Creator. There is a simple grandeur in this view of life with its several powers of growth, reproduction and of sensation, having been originally breathed into matter under a few forms, perhaps into only one, and that whilst this planet has gone cycling onwards according to the fixed laws of gravity and whilst land and water have gone on replacing each other—that from so simple an origin, through the selection of infinitesimal varieties, endless forms most beautiful and most wonderful have been evolved."

Then, in the first edition of 1859, the second sentence was omitted and third sentence had been reduced to: "There is grandeur in this view of life, with its several powers, having been originally breathed into a few forms or into one; and that, whilst this planet has gone circling on according to the fixed law of gravity, from so simple a beginning endless forms most beautiful and most wonderful have been, and are being evolved." A year later, however, in the second edition, the words "by the Creator" had been inserted after "breathed," presumably as a sop to his critics.

Darwin became first an agnostic and then an atheist, but "from the . . . impossibility of conceiving this immense and wonderful universe . . . [as] the results of blind chance or necessity . . . I feel compelled to look to a First Cause having an intelligent mind in some degree analogous to that of man: and [therefore] I deserve to be called a Theist."[4] As the essays presented here show, today a deist can both accept the facts and theories of evolutionary biology and still believe in God without the slightest inconsistency. A deist can accept that evolution proceeds by the operation of natural, material laws but nonetheless reserve the position that God was the original creative power (a slightly more conventional view would be that he also established those laws). The belief in a supreme being then allows someone, as Miller puts it, "to see a sense of order, meaning, and purpose in existence" beyond the blind chance and necessity (adherence to natural laws) of Darwin, and of Epicurus before him. Krauss here offers a similar conciliatory note: "Science may be viewed by some as a threat to faith, but as long as religious faith remains a core part of organized human society—and I don't foresee that as changing in the near future—science can play a key role in actually enriching this faith. . . . Anyone who believes [that there is a divine plan for how the world works] should recognize that by learning about nature one can come closer to understanding its ultimate meaning."

Both Krauss and Miller insist that this position is

different from the natural theology so popular in the seventeenth and eighteenth centuries (described in the essay by Numbers). Natural theology waned because, while it was easy to ascribe to God the appearances of beauty and perfect adaptation in the natural world, elements like death, evil, famine, and pestilence were not so easily explained as part of God's purpose for humanity. William Paley got around the problem by attributing every good thing to God and everything bad as a natural result of the operations of the laws he had set in progress—the "oeconomy of nature" that Alfred Lord Tennyson saw as "red in tooth and claw" and Darwin, ten years later, formalized as the struggle for existence.[5] Michael Behe and others have tried to revive natural theology in the form of a thesis of an irreducible complexity in nature that turns out (as Miller has so cogently shown here and elsewhere) to be reducible after all.[6] Scientific proof of God's hand in the act of creation remains as elusive as ever. As for the perfection of nature, anyone with impacted wisdom teeth or a bad sacroiliac will know that the human frame is merely a work in progress.

Experience suggests that even if a scientific proof of the origin of life from nonlife by purely material means were to be demonstrated in a laboratory experiment, there would still be a huge number of people who would say, "Yes, but that doesn't mean that God didn't do it first," or that "God has guided us to see how to do it now." The opposition to the teaching of evolution in schools does not, by and large, come from deists because they are not threatened by it. Science's great threat is to the more fundamentalist kinds of religion where the hand of God is more immediate. As long as the deist position continues to be a minority one, the question will necessarily remain, and not in the form "what is the debate?" or "why does it continue?" but rather, "how shall we deal with the fact that the debate inevitably *will* continue?"

If science and religion cannot reach a satisfactory accommodation of views, the next position is surely to develop something of the respectful mutual understanding that Hume hoped for.[7] Religion is too important in too many people's lives to be dismissed in the name of science. And the reverse is also true.

But how can there be understanding and respect when the general level of literacy is so low? One tactic of the creationist camp has been to try to dilute the teaching of science in schools. Only 7 percent of American adults are scientifically literate anyway. More than half believe that the sun orbits the earth. Thirty-four percent of Americans believe in ghosts, 34 percent believe in UFOs, and 24 percent believe in witches. Someone has done the creationists' work for them!

Sadly, the data for the religious side are not much better. A whopping 92 percent of the population claims to believe in God, 82 percent believe in miracles, the same percentage believes in an afterlife, and more than 30 percent believe that the Bible is the literal word of God. However, only half can name all four Gospels, and fewer know the name of the first book of the Old Testament, the ultimate authority for the act of God in Creation.[8]

The United States is a place where fairness and freedom of expression are taken very, very seriously, and "people" understand that far more clearly than they do the details of the religious and scientific questions actually at issue. Attacks on religion like those of Richard Dawkins or, more than two centuries ago, Thomas Paine, will not make it go away. Misrepresenting, or trying to suppress, any part of science will not succeed either. We must be able to disagree with the other's point of view without trying to discredit it and its practitioners.

The real enemy is ignorance and can only be addressed where religion and science are taught and discussed equally rigorously and separately, in schools and elsewhere. That is how we can approach the goals of the Terry Lectures: the convergence of religion and science for human welfare while Hume's "reasonable men" are "allowed to differ." A key role for scientists, therefore, should be to insist that students in school learn effectively, thoroughly, and impartially about religion.[9] Religionists might then come to feel safe in encouraging the open teaching of all aspects of science. Meanwhile, the 2,000-year-old debate will continue inevitably to be driven by our parallel searches for a secular grace arising from understanding the material world and for divinely inspired glimpses of the transcendent and mysterious.

Aggressors, Victims, and Peacemakers
Historical Actors in the Drama of
Science and Religion

RONALD L. NUMBERS

Talk of the relations between "science" and "religion" first became audible in the early 1800s, about the time that students of nature began referring to their work as science rather than natural philosophy (or natural history). Because natural philosophy allowed its practitioners, in the words of Isaac Newton, to discourse about God "from the appearances of things," one searches almost in vain for references to "natural philosophy and religion." Some writers expressed concern about tension between faith and reason, but they never pitted religion against science.[1]

The nineteenth century had barely begun, however, when the American Samuel Miller offered one of the earliest assessments of the relationship between religion and science. Despite finding during the past century "an unprecedented number of attacks on Revealed Religion, through the medium of science," the Presbyterian clergyman-historian believed that he was now living in "THE AGE OF CHRISTIAN SCIENCE." And so it seemed. "Many of the discoveries made in mechanical and chemical philosophy, during this period, have served to elucidate and confirm various parts of the Christian Scriptures," he wrote. "Every sober and well-directed inquiry into the natural history of man, and of the globe we inhabit, has been found to corroborate the Mosaic account of the Creation, the Fall, the Deluge, the Dispersion, and other important events recorded in the sacred volume."[2]

By this time both science and religion were taking on novel meanings. Science (*scientia* in Latin), long synonymous with knowledge generally, was rapidly coming to signify knowledge of nature in particular. The concept of "religion" was almost as new, having taken on its current meaning only during the Enlightenment. In the early years of the nineteenth century the phrase "science and religion" occasionally appeared as a synonym for culture generally—as in "the friends of science and religion"—but not until the 1820s and 1830s did books and articles feature the phrase "science and religion" in their titles, a sure sign that the authors were coming to view the two enterprises as independent if related. Perhaps the first English-language book with the phrase in its title came out in 1823, when Thomas Dick published his widely read *The Christian Philosopher; or, The Connection of Science and Philosophy with Religion*. By mid-century the conjunctive phrase was becoming a literary staple, and during the 1850s and 1860s several colleges and seminaries established professorships devoted to demonstrating (and pre-serving) the harmony of science and revealed religion.[3]

The most distinguishing characteristic of science was its insistence on using only natural explanations to account for the workings of nature, regardless of the personal beliefs of its practitioners. Since antiquity students of nature had expressed a reluctance to invoke the supernatural or miraculous, but only in the late eighteenth century did men of science begin insisting on it. One of the most ardent proponents of this methodology was Georges-Louis Leclerc, comte de Buffon, a prominent natural historian and cosmogonist in eighteenth-century France. Buffon called for a renunciation of all appeals to the supernatural. Those studying physical subjects, he argued, "ought as much as possible, to avoid having recourse to supernatural causes." Philosophers—that is, natural philosophers—"ought not to be affected by causes which seldom act, and whose action is always sudden and violent. These have no place in the ordinary course of nature. But operations uniformly repeated, motions which succeed one another without interruption, are the causes which alone ought to be the foundation of our reasoning." Buffon professed not to care whether such explanations were true, as long as they appeared probable. A theist, though not a practicing Christian, Buffon acknowledged, for example, that the Creator had originally set the planets in motion but considered the fact of no value to the natural philosopher.[4]

As early as 1800 a contributor to the *Medical Repository*, America's first medical magazine, applauded the growing tendency to refrain from invoking divine intervention in explaining the workings of nature, noting that "the modesty of science has given up the investigation of the first cause as beyond its comprehension." While acknowledging that some events might have resulted from "an immediate act of Deity," the anonymous author believed that "we should not dignify this [kind of explanation] with the name either of philosophy, science, or even of history." Yale's evangelical Benjamin Silliman, founder of the *American Journal of Science,* unashamedly embraced the rule of limiting scientific explanations to physical causes known to exist in nature. "Our advancement in natural science is not dependent upon our faith," he wrote in 1842. "All the problems of physical science are worked out by laborious examination, and strict induction."[5]

Such enthusiasm for banishing supernaturalism from science was possible only because Christian men of science typically attributed the laws of nature that they discovered to God. Thus naturalized science continued testifying to God's existence. Nevertheless, the practice of such methodological naturalism did not meet with universal approbation. "Physical science, at the present day, investigates phenomena simply as they are in themselves," observed a contributor to the *Biblical Repertory and Princeton Review.* "This, if not positively atheistic, must be of dangerous tendency. Whatever deliberately omits God from the universe, is closely allied to that which denies him."[6]

During the early decades of the nineteenth century writer after writer celebrated the delicious harmony between science and religion. Much of this doxological literature took the form of natural theology, which, in the words of the popular expositor the Anglican archdeacon William Paley, featured "evidences of the existence and attributes of the Deity, collected from the appearances of nature." For decades Paley and his watchmaker God became synonymous with natural theology. In the works of Paley and other natural theologians no natural object gave rise to more theological wonderment than the stunningly complex eye. "Were there no example in the world of contrivance except that of the *eye*," Paley insisted, "it would be alone sufficient to support . . . the necessity of an intelligent Creator."[7]

Despite its unsavory link to the natural religion of Enlightenment infidelity, early nineteenth-century Christians embraced the notion that nature revealed God. After all, even the Bible testified that "the heavens declare the glory of God" (Psalms 19:1). The venerated doctrine of God's two books—nature and the Bible—reinforced this conviction. In surveying the terrain occupied by "the religion of geology," the American preacher-naturalist Edward Hitchcock reported discovering no traces of "the barren mountains of scepticism and the putrid fens and quagmires of infidelity and atheism." Although geological discoveries had toppled notions of the recent appearance of life on earth and of a universal deluge, he assured readers that "no where in the whole world of science do we find regions where more of the Deity is seen in his works." Indeed, he insisted that "*scientific truth, rightly understood, is religious truth.*"[8]

Christian men of science stressed their religious contributions as much, it seems, to enhance the public image of science as to establish a metaphysical claim. In the workaday world of science, in the field and in the laboratory, natural theology played a miniscule role. Following up on Ralph Waldo Emerson's call for a "metaphysics of conchology," the historian Neal C. Gillespie tracked down over 135 books and articles written before 1859 by more than sixty British and American conchologists. Despite the amazing architecture and beauty of the shells, few of the naturalists alluded to the argument from design. This finding led Gillespie to conclude that well before Darwin's notorious attack on intelligent design, "natural theology of any kind, despite its strong grip on men's minds as a world view, had virtually ceased to be a significant part of the day-to-day practical explanatory structure of natural history."[9]

Early nineteenth-century American theologians nevertheless tended to view science as a bulwark against infidelity. "As the cavils and objections of infidels have been more readily answered as *natural science* has been enlarged," declared one Presbyterian theologian, "that branch of knowledge should form a part of that fund of information, which every minister of the Gospel should possess."[10]

Scientific Challenges

In the middle third of the nineteenth century some observers began to suspect that "every new conquest achieved by science involved the loss of a domain to religion." Especially disturbing were scientific efforts to reinterpret the first chapters of the Bible. During the three decades between about 1810 and 1840 men of science pushed successfully to replace the supernatural creation of the solar system with the nebular hypothesis, to expand the history of life on earth from 6,000 to millions of years, and to shrink Noah's flood to a regional event in the Near East. Many Christians readily adjusted their reading of the Bible to accommodate such findings; a mid-century observer surmised that only about "one half of the Christian public" continued to insist on the recent appearance of life on earth.[11]

Leading the effort to reconcile Genesis and geology was Benjamin Silliman. In 1833 he published an American edition of Robert Bakewell's *Introduction to Geology,* to which he appended a seventy-seven-page supplement in which he attempted to harmonize the findings of geological ages with the Mosaic account of a six-day creation and a universal deluge at the time of Noah. To accomplish this, Silliman divided the earth's development into six epochs, each corresponding to a "day," but not a period of twenty-four hours. He retained Noah's flood but limited it to superficial work, thus depriving it of its former role in burying the fossils found in the successive strata of rocks. "We find that the geological formations are in accordance with the Mosaic account of the creation; but more time is required for the necessary events of the creation than is consistent with the common understanding of the days," he concluded. "The history therefore is true, but it must be understood so as to be consistent with itself and with the facts."[12]

Because Bakewell's text served as the standard in the field, Silliman's views achieved wide circulation. But his effort at mediation exposed him to fire from three camps: biblical literalists who thought he had taken too many liberties with God's word, unbelieving men of science who thought God's word had no place in scientific discussions, and experts in biblical studies who thought that geologists should stick to what they actually knew and quit meddling in other disciplines. Typical of the first group was the Reverend Gardiner Spring, an old acquaintance of Silliman's from Yale and a fellow Calvinist, unhappy with the professor for assigning an early date to the creation, which Spring regarded as "a great *miracle*," incapable of being explained scientifically. "The collision is not between the Bible & *Nature*, but between the Bible & *natural philosophers*," he wrote Silliman, noting that his New Haven friend would probably think him "very ignorant, quite prejudiced, & not a little presumptuous." Spring, and others who read their Bibles literally, feared that if the geologists' history of the earth proved true, then the book of Genesis must be false.[13]

From South Carolina College the free-thinking Thomas Cooper, the first American openly to denounce religion as "the great enemy of Science," dashed off an entire booklet chastising Silliman for his "absolute unconditional surrender of his common sense to clerical orthodoxy." Cooper, nationally notorious as a "confirmed Infidel," had resigned the presidency of South Carolina College after quarreling with the state legislature over his opinion that "the Bible is in many respects a detestable, and in all respects an unauthenticated book." Cooper, who continued to teach geology at the college, expressed irritation that Silliman had "come out in full theological garb" in his supplement, which Cooper considered "a most injudicious attempt to intermingle what the peace of mankind requires to be kept separate." It was high time, Cooper concluded, "to resist the intermeddling of the clergy and their devoted adherents in matters of science."[14]

Moses Stuart, professor of sacred literature at An-dover Theological Seminary, faulted Silliman for over-stepping his area of scholarly expertise. A close friend of Silliman's from their student days together in New Haven, Stuart had once entertained the possibility of a career in science and mathematics. Instead he became the country's leading linguist, mastering Greek and Hebrew and learning Syriac, Aramaic, Arabic, and German. His fluency in German allowed him to read the early works of "higher criticism," which treated the Bible more as history and literature than as God's literal words. When Silliman first told Stuart that modern geological discoveries necessitated reading the "days" of Genesis as ages, the linguist, who had invested as much effort learning ancient languages as Silliman had learning science, resented his friend's arrogance in assuming the right to interpret ancient texts. "I am unable to see how the discoveries of modern science and of recent data can determine the meaning of Moses' words," observed Stuart a few years later. "Nothing can be more certain that that the sacred writers did not compose their books with modern science in view." In 1829, no doubt with Silliman in mind, he wrote that "the Bible was not designed to teach the Hebrews astronomy or geology." Hence a "day" for Moses presumably meant a twenty-four-hour period, not a vast geological age. "If Moses . . . contradicts geology, then be it so; but to violate the laws of exegesis in order to accommodate a geological theory . . . is not acting in accordance with the precepts of Scriptural Hermeneutics." Later Stuart lashed out at the presumption of scientific men like Silliman. "The digging of rocks and the digging of Hebrew roots," he noted, "are not as yet precisely the same operation."[15]

Silliman's attempt at peacemaking provoked real, even bitter, controversy, but it did not precipitate a battle in the so-called war between science and religion. The Silliman-Cooper exchange featured two of the nation's most prominent men of science disagreeing about the place of revelation in teaching geology. Silliman, Gardiner, and Stuart—all Calvinists—shared a heartfelt commitment to the sovereignty of God and the inspiration of the Bible. Silliman and Gardiner differed as fellow believers over the correct reading of scripture. Silliman and Stuart argued over the geological community's annoying habit of anachronistically reading modern science into ancient biblical texts and ignoring disciplinary boundaries. Eager to demonstrate their worth religiously as well as practically, geologists such as Silliman naively encroached on the domain of highly trained biblical scholars, just as intent on protecting their academic turf from interlopers as the geologists were.[16]

Increasing Tension

Silliman, like many of his scientific contemporaries, simultaneously sought the freedom to interject himself into the world of biblical exegesis while denying theologians and clergymen the right to monitor science. Such an arrangement could only embitter the clergy. Princeton Theological Seminary's Charles Hodge, a towering presence in mid-century American Calvinism, resented the marginalization of theologians from science. Although he continued to venerate men of science who disclosed "the wonderful works of God," by the late 1850s he was growing increasingly frustrated by their tendency to treat theologians who expressed themselves on scientific subjects as "trespassers" who should mind their own business. He attributed the growing "alienation" between men of science and men of the cloth in part to the former's "assumption of superiority" and their practice of stigmatizing their religious critics "as narrow-minded, bigots, old women, Bible worshippers, etc." He resented the lack of respect frequently shown to religious men, who were instructed by their scientific colleagues to quit meddling in science, while they themselves belittled religious beliefs and values. At times Hodge worried that science, devoid of religion, was becoming downright "satanic." He had no doubt that religion was in a "fight for its life against a large class of scientific men."[17]

Hodge especially worried about the efforts of some ethnologists in the 1840s and 1850s to replace the biblical story of Adam and Eve with a scientific account of multiple human creations, one for each race. Emboldened by the success of astronomers and geologists in freeing their disciplines from the shackles of scripture, a small group of American anthropologists launched an offensive to sever human history from its biblical roots. The effort began in the late 1830s, when the highly respected Philadelphia naturalist-physician Samuel George Morton published *Crania Americana* (1839). Already famous for his pathbreaking work on vertebrate paleontology in America, Morton drew on his incomparable collection of human skulls to argue for the independent origin of the human races. Because racial differences could be seen in the most ancient skulls, he eventually concluded that God must have created each racial group separately.[18]

Morton soon enlisted two rabid supporters of this

polygenist theory: George R. Gliddon, the United States vice-consul at Cairo, who collected Egyptian skulls for him, and Josiah Clark Nott, a physician from Mobile, Alabama. Nott, who had studied with the skeptical Thomas Cooper at South Carolina College, insisted that the Bible showed "no knowledge beyond the *human* knowledge of the day." In 1854 Nott and Gliddon brought out a massive 738-page treatise, *Types of Mankind*, devoted to the propagation of the multiple origin of humans, the "last great battle between science and dogmatism." Among the contributors was America's foremost naturalist, the Swiss-born Louis Agassiz.[19]

Nott and Gliddon's high-decibel attack on the "unity of man" provoked a spirited response from many members of the clergy, who viewed the polygenist assault as the closest to a battle "against the inspiration of the scriptures, pitched upon the ground of the natural sciences," seen in the pre–Civil War period. Hodge, who had readily accommodated the findings of geology and astronomy to his conservative theology, fretted that the same openness could not be applied to anthropology, because "the very object of the Bible was to clear up the history of the fall of man, to explain the condition in which he is found, and to reveal a plan for his recovery."[20]

On the heels of the polygenism attack came a sensational little book called *Vestiges of the Natural History of Creation* (1844). Issued anonymously by a British author, later identified as the Edinburgh publisher Robert Chambers, *Vestiges* wove together threads from the nebular hypothesis, historical geology, the evolutionary theory of Jean Baptiste Lamarck, and phrenology into a unified, if speculative, history of creation. It created an uproar on both sides of the Atlantic and brought, in the words of one historian, "an evolutionary vision of the universe into the heart of everyday life." Although Chambers denied dispensing with the Creator, critics thought otherwise. The teaching of *Vestiges*, fumed the Greek scholar Tayler Lewis, is nothing but "atheism—blank atheism, cold, cheerless, heartless, atheism." This outburst led one reader to complain that "a more rabid tirade can scarcely be found this side of the Middle Ages, & the smell of roast heretic is truly overpowering throughout." Another American reviewer charged the author of *Vestiges* with maintaining "a theory which virtually annihilates religion and gives us a universe without God." More than any other work antedating Darwin's *Origin of Species*, *Vestiges* introduced Americans to the notion of *development*, the term then used for what later came to be known as *evolution*.[21]

The spread of such "infidel" science caused many Christians, both conservatives and liberals, to feel under attack. According to the southern intellectual George Frederick Holmes, "The struggle between science and religion, between philosophy and faith, has been protracted through centuries; but it is only within recent years that the breach has become so open and avowed as to be declared by many to be irreconcilable." Science, predicted the Unitarian Andrew Preston Peabody in 1864, would become "the Armageddon—the final battlefield—in the conflict with infidelity."[22]

Religious fears spiked with the publication of Charles Darwin's *On the Origin of Species* (1859), in which the British naturalist sought "to overthrow the dogma of separate creations" and extend the domain of natural law throughout the organic world. Although Darwin initially remained silent about the application of his theory to humans, many readers immediately saw where he was heading. Twelve years later, in the *The Descent of Man* (1871), Darwin surprised few people when he finally came clean on human ancestry:

> Man is descended from a hairy quadruped, furnished with a tail and pointed ears, probably arboreal in its habits, and an inhabitant of the Old world. This creation, if its whole structure had been examined by a naturalist, would have been classed among the Quadrumana, as surely as would the common and still more ancient progenitor of the Old and new World monkeys. The Quadrumana and all the higher mammals are probably derived from an ancient marsupial animal, and this through a long line of diversified forms, either from some reptile-like, or some amphibian-like creature, and this again from some fish-like animal.

By this time Darwinism, in the words of the president of the American Association for the Advancement of Science, was "shaking the moral and intellectual world as by an earthquake."[23]

Some of Darwin's disciples tried to soften the blow to cherished religious beliefs—and common sense—by offering a theory of divine selection. The Harvard botanist Asa Gray, Darwin's closest American colleague, proposed that the inexplicable organic variations on which natural selection acted be attributed to divine providence. He also urged a "special origination" in connection with the appearance of humans and perhaps "for the formation of organs, the making of eyes, &c." Christian apologists had long regarded the intricate design of the eye as "a cure for atheism," and Darwin himself had readily conceded his vulnerability on this point. "To suppose that the eye, with all its inimitable contrivances for adjusting the focus to different distances . . . could have been formed by natural selection, seems, I freely confess, absurd in the highest possible degree," he wrote in the *Origin of Species*. But logical consistency impelled him to extend "the principle of natural selection to such startling lengths." When Gray forthrightly described the section of the *Origin* dealing with the making of the eye as "the weakest point in the book," Darwin confided that "the eye to this day gives me a cold shudder."[24]

Some conservative Christians judged Gray harshly for capitulating to Darwinism, while Darwin himself dismissed the American's supernatural solutions as scientifically unhelpful. In *The Variation of Animals and Plants under Domestication* (1868) Darwin noted that he could not "follow Professor Asa Gray in his belief that 'variation has been led along certain beneficial lines.'" Darwin's rejection of Gray's compromise, writes the historian Jon H. Roberts, "confirmed Protestant thinkers' suspicions that the Darwinian God was 'a cold and lifeless abstraction which could kindle no devotion in the soul' and clearly unmasked Darwin as yet another proponent of the naturalistic world view." It also prompted Charles Hodge, who had just recently referred to science and religion as the "twin daughters of heaven," to give his memorable verdict: "What is Darwinism? It is Atheism."[25]

Although a number of Christians called for "a truce... between the friends of Science and the friends of Religion," harmonizers, as Gray's experience illustrates, risked being caught in the crossfire between intransigent opponents of evolution and uncompromising defenders of Darwin. When the popular Brooklyn preacher Henry Ward Beecher argued for the compatibility of evolution and Christianity, the zoologist (and apostate Baptist) Edward Morse scoffed that such naive reconcilers failed to see that humanity's "origin from lower forms of life knocks in the head Adam and Eve, hence original sin, hence the necessity for vicarious atonement, hence everything that savors of the bad place." At the other end of the theological spectrum, one Christian antievolutionist railed against the "semi-Christian apologists" who tried to baptize evolution. Another went even further, suggesting that "the danger that the evolutionary hypothesis held for Christianity 'does not arise from the bold, arrogant speculations of atheistic scientists, but, rather, from the smooth and polished theistic believers, and teachers of science, who hold to evolution theories.' "[26]

Warfare

Throughout the middle third of the nineteenth century talk of harmony, not conflict, between science and religion prevailed in the Anglo-American world. Religious writers fearful of scientific aggression typically dismissed unwanted science as "science falsely so-called" or as "pseudo-science," allowing them to insist on their continuing affection for genuine science. Until the last decades of the century references to conflict commonly came from conservative religious leaders, fearful of, even angered, by the relentless incursions of science, genuine or false. Among intellectuals on both sides of the Atlantic the tone changed dramatically when, first, partisan historians of science and religion joined the debate and, second, when a group of hardcore "scientific naturalists" went out of their way to offend churchmen and to caricature organized religion as inimical to science.

In 1869 Andrew Dickson White, the young president of the proudly secular Cornell University, began rewriting history with an address in New York City on "The Battle-Fields of Science." Irritated by the criticism over his refusal to impose any religious tests on students and faculty and his declared intention of creating in Ithaca "an asylum for *Science*—where truth shall be sought for truth's sake, not stretched or cut exactly to fit Revealed Religion," the historian struck back. He depicted the religious struggle against science as "a war continued longer —with battles fiercer, with sieges more persistent, with strategy more vigorous than in any of the comparatively petty warfares of Alexander, or Caesar, or Napoleon." Although waged with pens rather than swords, and for minds rather than empires, this war, too, had destroyed lives and reputations. The combatants? Science and Religion. When "sweet reasonableness" failed to placate his critics, White fired his broadside, accusing them of possessing the same kind of narrow minds and mean spirits that had led to the persecution of Vesalius, Kepler, and Galileo. History showed, White declared, that "interference with Science in the supposed interest of religion—no matter how conscientious such interference may have been—has resulted in the direst evils both to Religion and Science, and *invariably.*"

To document this thesis, he surveyed "some of the hardest-fought battle-fields of this great war," illustrating how rigid biblical literalists and dogmatic theologians had stunted the growth of science and prostituted religion—only to lose in the end. In the following years, White delivered his lecture around the country and fleshed out his history of the conflict between science and religion with new illustrations, some drawn from contemporary hostilities between evolutionists and their foes. Finally, in 1896 he brought out a fully documented, two-volume *History of the Warfare of Science with Theology in Christendom.*[27]

Religious radicals and secularists loved White's inflammatory history. *The Outlook,* a liberal religious weekly, welcomed White's account of the struggle for "the liberty of learning and teaching." Each chapter, it said, "tells a similar story of province after province won by hard fighting," with the church using "terrorism and torture and every form of outrage on sensitive and truth-loving natures" to thwart the progress of science. Conservative Christians detested White's narrative, not only for its scolding tone but for its failure to acknowledge the support that Christianity had given to science over the centuries. Characteristically, White dismissed his opponents as "hysterics" and "zealots." His sole goal, he insisted, was "to find and to state, simply THE TRUTH."[28]

Nearly as influential as White in portraying Christianity as the aggressor in a war against science was another American, John William Draper, whose *History of the Conflict between Science and Religion* (1874) excoriated the Roman Catholic Church for its alleged suppression of science. According to one reviewer, Draper addressed "*the* question which is now agitating the world of thought." Indeed, he had. His book became an international best seller, going through fifty printings in a half-century in the United States and numerous translations worldwide. The Spanish edition fittingly won a spot on the Index of Prohibited Books. Catholics, not surprisingly, expressed outrage, describing it as "a farrago of falsehoods, with an occasional ray of truth." Orestes Brownson, a convert to Catholicism and one of the most outspoken critics of evolution in the United States, suggested that the book might better have been titled *The History of Events Which Never Happened*. Lumping Draper together with the scientific naturalists, Brownson accused his fellow American of a crime against humanity: "A thousand highway-robberies or a thousand cold-blooded murders would be but a light social offence in comparison with the publication of one such book as this before us."[29]

Enthusiastic support for this revisionist history came from White's and Draper's allies in Great Britain, led by the zoologist Thomas Henry Huxley and the Irish physicist John Tyndall. These unapologetically anticlerical scientists insisted that empirical, naturalistic science provided the *only* reliable knowledge of nature, humans, and society. They aimed less to naturalize science, which had largely been accomplished, than to create positions and influence for men such as themselves. They sought, as the historian Frank M. Turner has phrased it, "to expand the influence of scientific ideas for the purpose of secularizing society rather than for the goal of advancing science internally. Secularization was their goal; science, their weapon."[30]

Huxley, widely known as Darwin's bulldog for his aggressive advocacy of evolution, took the lead in associating Darwinism with skepticism. Resented in some quarters for his "bumptious air of omniscience," he was as early as 1859 publicly pitting science against religion and describing "science, and the methods of science," as "the masters of the world." At the same time he privately described "Theology & Parsondom" as "the natural & irreconcilable enemies of Science" and expressed the hope that he would live long enough to "see the foot of Science on the necks of her Enemies." In one of the most memorable similes to come out of the Darwinian debates, he wrote: "Extinguished theologians lie about the cradle of every science as the strangled snakes beside that of Hercules; and history records that whenever science and orthodoxy have been fairly opposed, the latter has been forced to retire from the lists, bleeding and crushed if not annihilated; scotched, if not slain." One Christian eager to harmonize Darwinism and religion worried that Huxley's "opposition to evangelical Christianity" would be felt "in every parish in the land." Given Huxley's immense popularity as a writer and lecturer in both Britain and America, such fears were not unwarranted.[31]

For centuries men of science had typically gone out of their way to assure religious people of their peaceful intentions, but Tyndall rivaled his good friend Huxley in provoking Christians to anger. In 1872 he captured the attention of the literate public with a scientific attack on miracles, particularly miracles of healing. In response to claims that intercessory prayer had saved the life of the typhoid-stricken Prince of Wales, Tyndall proposed an empirical test of the efficacy of prayer for healing. Religious leaders did not find this mockery amusing; they became outraged two years later when Tyndall used his platform as president of the British Association for the

Advancement of Science to deliver in Belfast what one Christian educator called "the boldest challenge which English-speaking theologians and philosophers had ever received from the materialist and atheist side." Two assertions in his notorious address attracted the most attention, and condemnation. At a time when most skeptical scientists still kept their doubts to themselves, Tyndall openly cast his lot with atheistic materialism, stating that matter possessed "the promise and potency of all terrestrial Life." He then declared all-out war on theology: "We claim, and we shall wrest from theology, the entire domain of cosmological theory. All schemes and systems which thus infringe upon the domain of science must, *in so far as they do this,* submit to its control, and relinquish all thought of controlling it. Acting otherwise proved disastrous in the past, and it is simply fatuous to-day." The expected "storm of opprobrium" broke out. When critics accused him of misusing his "position by quitting the domain of science, and making an unjustifiable raid into the domain of theology," he refused to apologize, noting instead that men of science had been successfully conquering theological land since the Middle Ages.[32]

Among those who stepped forward to defend the realm of the supernatural against "the advancing forces of science" was the devout English statesman William Gladstone. The sometime prime minister condemned the reprehensible practice of men such as Huxley and Tyndall "of first unduly narrowing the definition of Science, and then as unduly extending it to all the opinions which those persons think fit to hold, and all the theories they erect on the subject they term scientific." While regarding science "on her own ground" as invaluable, Gladstone

denounced the "Scientism" of the naturalists as "no better than an impudent impostor . . . [that] must expect like
other impostors to be detected & chastised." Huxley
treated harmonizing strategies with "unconcealed and
unmeasured scorn" (as Gladstone described it), dismiss-
ing "the reconcilers of Genesis with science" as the
"modern representatives of Sisyphus" and insisting that
he was not antagonistic "to religion, but to the heathen
survivals and the bad philosophy under which religion
herself is often well-nigh crushed." Science, he went on,
"takes for its province only that which is susceptible
of clear intellectual comprehension, and that outside the
boundaries of that province they must be content with
imagination, with hope, and with ignorance." Little wonder one observer concluded that Huxley was "not regarded with favor by churchmen generally."[33]

Although one would scarcely have gathered it from
the hubbub over the alleged war between science and
religion, harmonizers greatly outnumbered combatants,
even in the scientific community. In the mid-1870s, for
example, the Reverend Joseph Cook drew throngs to his
Monday lectures in Boston. "So far as I know it has no
exact precedent in our history," wrote one admirer. "A
strange sight it is, that of a thousand or more people
gathered every week at noonday to listen to elaborate
discussions of the most profound questions of science
and religion." As late as 1880 a Princeton astronomer
speculated "that only a small (but rather noisy) minority
[of scientists] were decidedly hostile to Christianity."
Nevertheless, the press focused on the handful of extreme
antagonists.[34]

At times, attacks on those who tried to reconcile science and religion became something of a Victorian spectator sport. When Gladstone's sometime associate George Campbell, the eighth Duke of Argyll, published a widely read book attributing the laws of nature to God, Huxley took him to task in the *Nineteenth Century*. In his "onslaught," reported an excited reader, Huxley "suddenly leaps on the Duke and knocks him down, and tramples on him, and rolls over him, and stones him to death,— with such a rollicking dare-devil legerdemain that there is nothing left of the titled humbug."[35]

Counterattacks

For decades opponents of Huxley's and Tyndall's "scientism," a term that came into currency in the 1870s, protested the imperialistic tendencies of science. These dissenters came largely from cultural elites in all walks of life. That changed dramatically in the 1920s, when fundamentalist Christians in the United States launched a populist crusade to eradicate evolution from the churches and schools of America. The Seventh-day Adventist "geologist" George McCready Price, described by *Science* as "the principal scientific authority of the Fundamentalists," spelled out the woeful implications of evolution for religion and society. "Do you know," he asked in words reminiscent of the anti-Christian zoologist Morse over a half-century earlier, "that the theory of evolution absolutely does away with God and with His Son Jesus Christ, and with His revealed Word, the Bible, and is largely responsible for the class struggle now endangering the world?" Price was far from alone in his dire assessment. In 1923 leaders of the Holiness movement

denounced Darwinism as "Satan's greatest and most subtle form of attack upon the faith of the world in the fact of
the supernatural, the deity of Christ, the inspiration of
the Scriptures and the instantaneity of salvation." Given
the threat, no Christian preacher worth his pulpit could
stand by idly while the advocates of evolution "invaded
his realm."[36]

At times the rhetoric, on both sides, became over-
heated. "Next to the fall of Adam and Eve," proclaimed
one Mississippi fundamentalist, "Evolution and the teaching of Evolution in tax-supported schools is the greatest
curse that ever fell upon this earth." The acerbic journalist
H. L. Mencken, reporting from Dayton, Tennessee, in
1925, warned that the campaign against evolution "serves
notice on the country that Neanderthal man is organizing
in these forlorn backwaters of the land, led by a fanatic
[Bryan], rid of sense and devoid of conscience." Like
Mencken, some science teachers displayed what the mod-
ernist theologian Shailer Mathews described as "a 'smart
Alec attitude' toward religion." Academic freedom, he
advised, did not grant teachers "license to insult other
people's convictions."[37]

Despite their antipathy toward Darwinism—to say
nothing of Freudianism, behaviorism, and scientism generally—few fundamentalists saw themselves as opponents
of science. Like critics of Christianity who professed admiration for religion while damning theology and religious organizations, fundamentalists typically stressed
their great love of science. It is an "unquestioned fact,"
avowed the Reverend William Bell Riley, founder of the
World's Christian Fundamentals Association, "that evolution is not a science; it is a hypothesis only, a specu-

lation." Another fundamentalist leader insisted: "It is not 'science' that orthodox Christians oppose. No! no! a thousand times, No! They are opposed only to the theory of evolution, which has not yet been proved, and therefore is not to be called by the sacred name of *science*." Although the antievolutionists failed to convince more than a few states to ban the teaching of human evolution, they succeeded in casting a pall over evolution education for decades to come.[38]

The following three decades, plagued by a global depression and a second world war, saw relatively little action on the science-and-religion front, at least not much that attracted the attention of the news media. The outside world paid little attention to the activities of the evangelical American Scientific Affiliation (founded in 1941) or the liberal Institute on Religion in an Age of Science (1954), both of which played mediating roles in the Christian community. Even the Moody Institute of Science's hugely successful series of films on the harmony of God's two books, nature and the Bible, viewed by millions and shown by the United States Air Force to servicemen around the globe, provoked little criticism.[39]

In the educational arena advocates of evolution remained on the defensive until the late 1950s, when the centennial of the publication of *Origin of Species* emboldened biologists to mount a counterattack, rallying to the slogan "One Hundred Years without Darwin Are Enough." Fortunately for them, an opportunity to do something about the eclipse of Darwinism was opening up. In reaction to the embarrassing launch of Sputnik by the Soviet Union in 1957, the U.S. government generously funded the rewriting of science textbooks, hoping

thereby to catch up with the Russians. A group of biology educators used the newly available federal funds to
produce a series of high-school biology texts, known as
the Biological Sciences Curriculum Studies (BSCS), that
featured evolution. As evolution-filled textbooks flooded
classrooms in the 1960s, they incited a holy backlash
from conservative Christians, who saw this latest evolutionary offensive as an "attempt to ram evolution down
the throats of our children." In the opinion of one creationist biology teacher, the BSCS books were "dedicated
to the promulgation of total organic evolution to the ex-
clusion of objectivity in geology, if need be, in order
to eliminate any belief in fiat creation." The Berkeley-
trained creationist geneticist Walter E. Lammerts scato-
logically dismissed the BSCS texts as "mostly BS."[40]

Aggrieved Christian parents fought back, no longer
seeking to outlaw evolution, as fundamentalists had done
in the 1920s, but to make "creation science" the equal of
"evolution science." About the same time an internecine
battle broke out among evangelical Christians, as so-
called young-earth creationists, who squeezed the history of life of earth—and sometimes the history of the
entire universe—into no more than 10,000 years, under-
took an evangelistic campaign to wean believers away
from the accommodationist views of Bryan and others.
The leaders of the movement viewed evolution as a Satanic tool of atheism. Scientists and journalists scarcely
noticed this acrimonious battle among Bible-believing
Christians. But about 1980 open-minded Christians and
secularists became alarmed when the "creation scientists"
began urging state legislatures to require the teaching of
"creation science" (that is, young-earth creationism with-

out any mention of the Bible) whenever "evolution science" appeared in the classroom. The ensuing debate split the religious community, pitting conservative evangelicals, including fundamentalists and many Pentecostals, against mainstream and liberal Christians. Two states, Arkansas and Louisiana, passed balanced-treatment laws. In 1981 in Little Rock, in a subsequent trial over the Arkansas law, the fissure dividing Christians became clear. The plaintiffs, who opposed the teaching of creation science, included a host of Catholic, Protestant, and Jewish organizations, while the defendants recruited a number of scientists to testify on their behalf. The Protestant theologian Langdon Gilkey, who appeared for the plaintiffs, accurately characterized the contest as a battle between "liberal religion and liberal science on the one side, and absolutist religion and its appropriate 'science' on the others." Nevertheless, the press—and intellectuals generally—commonly caricatured the conflict in Little Rock as just another battle in the long warfare between science and religion.[41]

Intelligent Design

Soon after a Supreme Court decision in 1987 decisively ended the creationists' campaign for equal time, many antievolutionists pinned their hopes on something called intelligent design (ID). Setting aside the biblical accounts of creation, the partisans of ID, orchestrated by the Discovery Institute in Seattle, aimed to pitch a tent big enough to accommodate the majority of antievolutionists, regardless of religious belief. Above all, they sought to revolutionize the practice of science by allowing

supernatural explanations to count as genuine science. In
an iconoclastic little book called *Darwin on Trial* (1991),
which symbolically launched the ID crusade, a Berkeley
law professor, Phillip E. Johnson, took issue with the
assumption that scientists, when explaining the workings
of nature, should limit themselves to natural causes and
avoid supernatural explanations. This bias, he argued, unfairly limited the range of possible explanations and ruled
out any consideration of theistic factors. The Presbyterian lawyer especially targeted "methodological naturalism," which, unlike metaphysical naturalism, allowed
even conservative Christians to practice conventional science without compromising their religious convictions.
Rejecting this salutary approach, ID advocates boldly set
out "to reclaim science in the name of God."[42]

In 1996 one of Johnson's disciples, a Roman Catholic
biochemist named Michael Behe, brought out *Darwin's
Black Box,* in which he asserted that biochemistry had
"pushed Darwin's theory to the limit . . . by opening
the ultimate black box, the cell, thereby making possible
our understanding of how life works." The "astonishing
complexity of subcellular organic structure" led him to
conclude—on the basis of scientific data, he asserted, "not
from sacred books or sectarian beliefs"—that intelligent
design had been at work. The telltale signs of such activity were "irreducibly complex" organic structures,
such as the bacterial flagellum, which propels microscopic organisms—and which quickly replaced the eye as
the icon of design. IDers claimed to have found irrefutable *scientific* evidence of a godlike being. "The result is
so unambiguous and so significant that it must be ranked

as one of the greatest achievements in the history of science," Behe gushed. "The discovery [of intelligent design] rivals those of Newton and Einstein, Lavoisier and Schroedinger, Pasteur and Darwin"—and by implication elevated *its* discoverer to the pantheon of modern science.[43]

Behe and his ID colleagues derived their "evidence" for a designer from their inability to explain the origin of organisms naturally, an intellectual stance reminiscent of what Darwin once attributed to those who denied the evolution of humans: "Ignorance more frequently begets confidence than does knowledge: it is those who know little, and not those who know much, who so positively assert that this or that problem will never be solved by science."[44]

Although a few leading intellectuals, including the distinguished philosopher of religion Alvin Plantinga and Huston Smith, one of the world's leading experts on comparative religion, sided with the ID revolutionaries, most remained wary, if not downright hostile.[45] The attempt to portray old-fashioned natural theology as legitimate science, while at the same time marginalizing the "scientific creationists" for their divisive insistence on a particular reading of Genesis, stirred up a flurry of opposition. The majority of scientists either ignored ID or dismissed it as "the same old creationist bullshit dressed up in new clothes." The linguist Noam Chomsky described ID as "vacuous"—"about as interesting as 'I don't understand.'" One of the most spirited discussions of intelligent design and scientific naturalism took place among conservative Christian scholars. Having long since come to terms with doing science naturalistically, reported the editor of *Perspectives on Science and Christian Faith*, "most evangelical observers—especially working scientists—[remained] deeply skeptical." Though supportive of a theistic worldview, they balked at being "asked to add 'divine agency' to their list of scientific working tools."[46]

The creationist and intelligent-design attacks on evolution especially annoyed agnostics and atheists, who denounce their religious adversaries in language largely unheard since the days of Huxley and Tyndall. Reprising the roles of the two Victorians were the British biologist Richard Dawkins and the American philosopher Daniel Dennett. Dawkins, Britain's number-one public intellectual, repeatedly went out of his way to bait and belittle religious believers, especially creationists, whom he described as "ignorant, stupid or insane." To the consternation of even liberal Christians, Dawkins diagnosed religious faith "as a kind of mental illness" and as "the great cop-out, the great excuse to evade the need to think and evaluate evidence." On one occasion he described religious faith as "one of the world's great evils, comparable to the smallpox virus but harder to eradicate." In his elegantly written book *The Blind Watchmaker* (1986), hyped on the dust jacket as perhaps "the most important book on evolution since Darwin," he stressed the role of blind natural selection in creating organized complexity and denied any role to Paley's God. In an oft-quoted statement, he thanked Darwin for making "it possible to be an intellectually fulfilled atheist." God, he insisted in a best-selling book, was nothing but a "delusion." Recognizing Dawkins's similarities to Huxley, Darwin's bulldog, an admirer dubbed the Oxford evolutionist "Darwin's Rottweiler."[47]

Dawkins's attacks on ID brought it much undeserved publicity. As one Christian Scientist observed, Dawkins probably "single-handedly makes more converts to Intelligent Design than any of the leading Intelligent Design theorists." Even the objects of abuse sometimes reveled in the attention they received. William Dembski, a leader of the ID camp, sent the following note of appreciation to Dawkins: "I know that you personally don't believe in God, but I want to thank you for being such a wonderful foil for theism and for intelligent design more generally. In fact, I regularly tell my colleagues that you and your work are one of God's greatest gifts to the intelligent-design movement. So please, keep at it!"[48]

In *Darwin's Dangerous Idea* (1995), which Dawkins warmly endorsed, Dennett portrayed Darwinism as "a universal solvent, capable of cutting right to the heart of everything in sight"—and particularly effective in dissolving religious beliefs. Creationists would have cheered his characterization of Darwinism, but certainly not his description of them. He despised creationists, arguing that "there are no forces on this planet more dangerous to us all than the fanaticisms of fundamentalism." Displaying a degree of intolerance more characteristic of a fanatical fundamentalist than an academic philosopher, he called for "caging" those who would deliberately misinform children about the natural world, just as one would cage a threatening wild animal. "The message is clear," he wrote: "those who will not accommodate, who will not temper, who insist on keeping only the purest and wildest strain of their heritage alive, we will be obliged, reluctantly, to cage or disarm, and we will do our best to disable the memes [traditions] they fight for."[49]

Dawkins and Dennett, though representing a minority view, were not alone in displaying hostility toward religion. A sample of the widely circulated quips includes the following:

> *Francis Crick* (winner of the Nobel Prize for co-discovering the structure of DNA): The view of ourselves as "persons" is just as erroneous as the view that the Sun goes around the Earth. . . . In the fullness of time, educated people will believe there is no soul independent of the body, and hence no life after death.

> *Peter Atkins* (University of Oxford chemist): Science is often considered to be arrogant in abrogating to itself, in the eyes of some (my own included), the claim to be the sole route to true, complete, and perfect knowledge.

> *Edward O. Wilson* (entomologist and sociobiologist at Harvard University): The final decisive edge enjoyed by scientific naturalism will come from its capacity to explain traditional religion, its chief competition, as a wholly material phenomenon. Theology is not likely to survive as an independent intellectual discipline.

> *William B. Provine* (biologist and historian of science at Cornell University): Let me summarize my views on what modern evolutionary biology tells us loud and clear. . . . There are no gods, no purposes, no goal-directed forces of any kind. There is no life after death. . . . There is no ultimate foundation for ethics, no ultimate meaning to life, and no free will for humans, either.

Perhaps the most famous, or notorious, of all such statements was the celebrity astronomer Carl Sagan's opening line in his Public Broadcasting System (PBS) series *Cosmos:* "The cosmos is all there is or ever was or ever will be."[50]

Such imperialistic statements caused many in the scientific community, even unbelievers, to squirm. In the United States, where nearly 90 percent of the population identified as theists, it only made sense not to equate science, and especially evolution, with atheism. Besides, if the godless joined fundamentalists in labeling evolution atheistic, they might make it impossible to teach evolution without violating the constitutionally mandated separation of church and state.

In the late 1990s Stephen Jay Gould attempted to calm the waters agitated by the scientific atheists on the left and the antievolutionists on the right. The Harvard paleontologist possessed excellent credentials to serve as peacemaker: he was not only one of the best-known scientists in the world but a nonobservant Jew and a longtime critic of creationism. Without naming the miscreants, he confessed to getting "discouraged when some of my colleagues tout their private atheism (their right, of course, and in many ways my own suspicion as well) as a panacea for human progress against an absurd caricature of 'religion,' erected as a straw man for rhetorical purposes." Repudiating the notion of inevitable conflict, as well as syncretistic endeavors, he allied himself with the "people of goodwill" who "wish to see science and religion at peace, working together to enrich our practical and ethical lives." His solution was to think of science and religion as occupying two nonoverlapping cultural spaces or "magisteria." According to this scheme, science would try "to document the factual character of the natural world, and to develop theories that coordinate and explain these facts," while religion would restrict itself to the "realm of human purposes, meanings, and values." Unfortunately, this prescription for peace failed to satisfy the most interested parties.[51]

Another aspiring peacemaker from the evolutionist camp was the philosopher of science Michael Ruse, whose testimony at the Little Rock trial in 1981 had guided the judge in his determination of "creation science" as unscientific. An uncompromising and sometimes feisty agnostic, Ruse had been sufficiently influenced by the Quakerism of his youth to strive for peaceful coexistence between Christianity and science. His irenic attitude inspired one writer, unable to resist another dog metaphor, to call him "Darwin's cocker-spaniel." In a book called *Can a Darwinian Be a Christian?* Ruse answered his query with a resounding "Absolutely!" Although he saw no reason why Darwinians should be Christians, he did think that they should "try to be understanding of those who are." He thought they should also try to understand the people they despised and not remain "pig ignorant" about religion, as he accused Dawkins of doing. Elsewhere Ruse took Dawkins, Dennett, and their ilk to task for turning biological evolution into a secular religion called "evolutionism," a metaphysical extrapolation from Darwin's scientific theory.[52]

Ruse fretted that Dawkins and Dennett were "making it very difficult for those of us who care about evolution to put forward a reasonable face to the reasonable portion [of the public] in the middle." In an e-mail exchange subsequently made public, Dennett offered his fellow philosopher some pseudo-friendly advice: "You may want to try to extricate yourself, since you are certainly losing ground fast in the evolutionary community that I am in touch with. . . . I . . . think you are doing a disservice to the case of taking science seriously." Ruse, proud of the decades he had devoted to promoting Darwinism and fighting creationism, replied:

> I am a hard-line Darwinian and always have been very publicly when it did cost me status and respect. . . . I think that you and Richard [Dawkins] are absolute disasters in the fight against intelligent design—we are losing this battle, not the least of which is the two new supreme court justices who are certainly going to vote to let it into classrooms—what we need is not knee-jerk atheism but serious grappling with the issues—neither of you are willing to study Christianity seriously and to engage with the ideas—it is just plain silly and grotesquely immoral to claim that Christianity is simply a force for evil, as Richard [Dawkins] claims—more than this, we are in a fight, and we need to make allies in the fight, not simply alienate everyone of good will.[53]

In the Sermon on the Mount Jesus blessed the peacemakers, promising that they would "be called sons of God" (Matthew 5:9). It did not work quite that way for Gould or Ruse, whom the religion-bashers accused being too generous to religion and conservative Christians criticized for marginalizing their concerns. As one of the latter said of Gould, his proposal was tantamount to offering believers "terms of surrender." The University of Chicago biologist and sometime Dawkins collaborator Jerry Coyne condescendingly dismissed reconciliation

projects as being especially appealing to "academics near-
ing the end of their careers." Naming Gould and Ruse, he
dismissed their attempts to reconcile science and religion
"because nearly all religions make claims about the real
world—the domain of science—that don't stand up to
scientific scrutiny." Dawkins, who liked to portray himself as the Winston Churchill of the war against religion,
dismissed Ruse as a leader of "the Neville Chamberlain
school of evolutionists," a reference to the British prime
minister who tried to mollify Adolf Hitler by giving him
Czechoslovakia. Dennett went even further, telling Ruse
that he feared the Florida State philosopher was "being
enlisted on side of the forces of darkness."[54]

Why Has the Debate Continued?

Despite the many controversies over science and religion,
it would be misleading to describe their relationship as a
war. The most intense conflicts, as we have seen, often
pitted Christian against Christian, scientist against scientist, skeptic against skeptic. Over the years most scientists, at least in the United States, have remained theists of
one kind or another, and religious organizations have fos-
tered science more frequently than they have inhibited it.
Fundamental to the intellectual skirmishes that did break
out was genuine, heartfelt disagreement: over the meaning of sacred texts, the boundaries of science, and the
implications of science for morality and worldviews. In
some instances irreconcilable epistemologies made harmony virtually impossible.[55]

Outsiders, such as journalists and politicians, have
often used the science-religion debates for their own

ends. The news media seem incapable of resisting the spectacle of scholars slanging one another and of impertinent critics challenging scientific orthodoxy. After more than a decade of effort the Discovery Institute proudly announced in 2007 that it had gotten some 700 doctoral-level scientists and engineers to sign "A Scientific Dissent from Darwinism." This number represented less than 0.023 percent of the world's scientists. But despite such miniscule support for intelligent design among practicing scientists and the virtual absence of peer-reviewed scientific publications supportive of ID, newspapers and magazines around the world have featured what *Time* called the "Evolution Wars." Some of this attention stemmed from the press's quest for "balance," regardless of merit. The conservative pundit Ann Coulter, who rarely strove for balance, once described Darwin's "single greatest victory" as coming "in the realm of rhetoric, not science." Had she been writing about the antievolutionists rather than Darwin, she would have been right on target. ID's single greatest victory was misleading the public and press into believing that a serious scientific controversy existed about the status of organic evolution.[56]

Political activists such as Coulter have done their best to fan the flames of controversy. When the ID theorist Jonathan Wells published *The Politically Incorrect Guide to Darwinism and Intelligent Design* (2006), Coulter, who in her own work described Darwinism as "about one notch above Scientology in scientific rigor," urged fellow right-wingers to "Annoy a godless liberal: buy this book!" Not all conservatives, to be sure, shared her sentiments. The psychiatrist-columnist Charles Krauthammer, for example, dismissed ID as a "farce" that "foolishly pits evolution against faith." Republican Judge John E. Jones III, who presided over the 2005 trial of the Dover, Pennsylvania, school board for promoting ID, described the actions of the school board as a "breathtaking inanity." In 2006 the Republican mayor of New York City, Michael R. Bloomberg, chastised fellow conservatives for disregarding scientific "facts that don't happen to agree with their agendas." Such "faith-based science," he argued, would more accurately be called "political science."[57]

Few politicians spoke so critically. Whether out of conviction or fear of losing votes, most politicians refrained from saying anything negative about ID. During the 2004 presidential campaign, for example, a reporter for the journal *Science* asked candidates George W. Bush and John F. Kerry whether " 'intelligent design' or other scientific critiques of evolutionary theory [should] be taught in public schools." Both deferred to local control, with the former adding that "Of course, scientific critiques of any theory should be a normal part of the science curriculum." A year later President Bush, who had been discussing ID in his weekly Bible study sessions at the White House, publicly endorsed the teaching of both design and evolution, as did some members of his cabinet and congressional leaders.[58]

At the turn of the twenty-first century the United States stood first in the world in its support for science. At the same time nearly two-thirds (65.5 percent) of the population regarded "creationism" as definitely or probably true, and more than eight out of ten expressed faith "in the healing power of personal prayer." Given these attitudes and the new issues constantly arising—from banning reproductive technologies and teaching about sex to saving the environment and conducting stem-cell research—there is little reason for believing that debates over science and religion will die down soon. Ominously, such debates, once confined largely to the United States, are now spreading rapidly around the globe.[59]

Darwin, God, and Dover
What the Collapse of "Intelligent Design" Means for Science and Faith in America

KENNETH R. MILLER

To many within academia, the notion of a "religion and science debate" seems to be the stuff of history.[1] It conjures up visions of papal courts and forbidden books, of nineteenth-century confrontations between reason and superstition in the halls of royal societies, of a world in which the value of science had yet to prove itself, even in the minds of the most learned members of society. It comes as somewhat of a shock, therefore, to realize that this debate is as contemporary as the last election, as far-reaching as the global village itself, and as important to the future of American society as any conflict without our culture today. Shock it may be, but all of this is true nonetheless.

Bleeding Kansas

We live, as the saying goes, in interesting times, and there
has been no better example of these times than the pivotal
midwestern state of Kansas. In 1999 the state's elected
Board of Education voted to remove key portions of the
theory of evolution from that state's Science Standards, as
well as critical elements of earth history and cosmology.[2]
Seen as an obvious attempt to weaken the teaching of
evolution and pave the way for the introduction of creationist ideas into the public school classroom, this move
was strongly opposed by state and national scientific and
educational organizations. These organizations joined
with a number of civic and professional groups within the
state to oppose pro-creationist board members at the bal-
lot box in the subsequent year and mounted an effective
campaign to support the election of pro-science members
to the Kansas board. Victory came in the summer of 2000
after a bitter primary election campaign and resulted in
the seating of a pro-science board that reversed the antievolution standards the next year.[3]

The electoral victories of pro-science candidates did
not end the controversy over evolution, however, and
determined opposition to evolution changed the com-
position of the board yet again in the 2004 elections. The
new board majority explored a number of strategies designed to weaken the teaching of evolution, including a
series of hearings in May of 2005 at which leading proponents of "intelligent design" (ID) argued that there is a
genuine scientific controversy over the validity of evolutionary theory, and that Kansas students should be taught
about this controversy. I should note, in the interest of

fair disclosure, that a number of scientists, myself included, who might have defended the theory of evolution
were invited to these hearings and chose not to come.
Realizing that the hearings were to be held in front of a
three-member board subcommittee of avowed evolution
opponents, I saw no reason to participate in what seemed
to be to be a frank attempt to generate political cover
for curriculum changes that the board was clearly determined to make regardless of the evidence presented to
them. Neither did organizations such as the American
Association for the Advancement of Science (AAAS),
which urged the scientific community not to participate.

The changes adopted by the Kansas Board of Education later in 2005 discarded the recommendations of their
own standards-writing committee and substituted a series of standards strongly supported by ID advocates.
These standards then became the focal point of political
activity in the next campaign, and once again pro-science
forces mounted an effective campaign throughout the
state, resulting in a 6–4 board majority after the 2006
elections.[4] Only time will reveal the next engagement in
the Kansas evolution wars, but there is little doubt that
these conflicts will continue. Students of history are
acutely aware of the battleground role that "bleeding
Kansas" played in the years before the American Civil
War, and even in the middle of this conflict it is only fair
to wonder if once again Kansas has become a burned-
over district in the rehearsal for a larger struggle affecting
all of American society. In an important sense this has
already taken place. And, very much like the Civil War,
the struggle reached its climax, if not its resolution, in a
small town in Pennsylvania.

Terms of the Battle

The opponents of evolution often claim to oppose what they call "Darwinism" because of its scientific flaws and weaknesses. Their own rhetoric, however, shows that they regard evolution as a powerful idea rather than a weak one, and they attribute to it many of the pervasive problems of modern society. A graphic image, distributed by Answers in Genesis, perhaps the largest and most far-reaching antievolution organization in the United States, shows evolution as the rock-solid foundation of nearly everything they regard as wrong with modern society. This image (Figure 1) depicts evolution as the root of such evils as "homosexual behavior," "pornography," and "abortion."

If Darwin's great idea is indeed seen as the foundation of everything wrong in society, including lawlessness, abortion, pornography, and the dissolution of marriage, then it must be opposed at all costs. Furthermore, any factual evidence that science might gather in favor of evolution must be disregarded in favor of the greater truth upon which all of society is founded. Such powerful motivations drive sincere and dedicated opposition to science and must not be underestimated.

The rhetoric of social decay is pervasive in the antievolution movement. When thirteen students were killed in the 1999 massacre at Columbine High School in Colorado, Representative Tom DeLay took to the floor of the House of Representatives to read a letter into the *Congressional Record.* That letter asserted that one of the true causes of this murderous tragedy was surely that "Our school systems teach the children that they are nothing

Meaning of Life	Abortion
Standards	Pornography
Marriage	Homosexual Behavior
Laws	Lawlessness
Creation	Evolution

FIGURE 1: Opponents of evolution see it as the foundation of social and political trends that they decry for moral and religious reasons. Redrawn from a graphic on the Answers in Genesis Web site (www.answersingenesis.org).

but glorified apes who have evolutionized out of some primordial soup of mud."[5] Pennsylvania Senator Rick Santorum, speaking on the National Public Radio program *Morning Edition* on August 4, 2005, characterized the struggle over evolution like this: "If we are the result of chance, if we're simply a mistake of nature, then that puts a different moral demand on us. In fact, it doesn't put a moral demand on us . . . than, if in fact we are a creation of a being that has moral demands." In other words, if evolution is right, there are no moral demands placed upon us—and society must be prepared to suffer the consequences.

In October 2006, speaking about a heated contest for a seat on Ohio's Board of Education, a talk show host identified as Pastor Ernie Sanders tried to clarify the issues in the race for the benefit of his listeners. Pointing to the contest between incumbent board member (and evolution opponent) Deborah Owens Fink and her pro-evolution challenger, Tom Sawyer, Reverend Sanders put it this way: "If you believe in God, creation and true science, vote for Debbie, . . . if you believe in evolution, abortion and sin, you've got Tom Sawyer, right?" Clearly, in the view of the antievolution movement, the stakes could not be higher.

"Intelligent Design" Comes to Dover

The pivotal battle in ID's war against evolution began, very much as the battle of Gettysburg did, with an almost incidental skirmish. In 2004 the science department at Dover Area High School in Dover, Pennsylvania, was allowed to choose new textbooks for their general biology classes, and they selected a book published by Prentice Hall, *Biology,* by Kenneth Miller and Joseph Levine. The first hint of trouble came when members of Dover's Board of Education balked at approving the textbook. One of the board's members complained that the book was "laced with Darwinism from beginning to end" and set about helping to present an alternative to teachers.[6] The board also arranged for the purchase of two classroom sets of the ID textbook *Of Pandas and People,* which were placed in the high school library.[7] What followed would lead to a First Amendment trial on the issues of evolution and intelligent design drawing worldwide press attention to the small town of Dover and to the continuing battle over science education in the United States.

On December 14, 2004, a group of eleven parents of students in the Dover school district filed a lawsuit in federal court alleging that the Dover Board of Education had violated their constitutional rights. *Kitzmiller v.*

Dover, as the lawsuit is known, charged that by using government power to bring the idea of "intelligent design" into public school classrooms, the board had, in effect, established a religion in violation of the First Amendment to the Constitution. The case moved toward trial with remarkable speed, and on September 25, 2005, Judge John E. Jones III called both sides to order in federal court in Harrisburg, Pennsylvania. I was called as lead witness for the plaintiffs and spent much of the first two days of the trial on the witness stand, making the case for evolution and being cross-examined by attorneys defending the school board.

The details of the trial have been widely reported, and a complete recounting of the proceedings is well beyond the scope of this chapter. Nonetheless, as the trial played out, events in the courtroom provided for exactly the sort of grand confrontation for which many partisans in the struggle had been hoping. Only four months earlier, William Dembski, one of the leading intellectuals of the ID movement, had fantasized about the opportunities that such a trial might present for ID in these words: "I therefore await the day when the hearings are not voluntary but involve subpoenas that compel evolutionists to be deposed and interrogated at length on their views. There are ways for this to happen, and the wheels are in motion. . . . What I propose, then, is a strategy for interrogating the Darwinists to, as it were, squeeze the truth out of them."[8]

Lest there be any doubt as to the intensity of the strategy Dr. Dembski had proposed, he included photographs in his blog entry of a Charles Darwin doll with its head placed firmly in a vise. Clearly the Dover trial was shaping up to be the decisive battle in which the ID movement would prove itself.

But a funny thing happened on the way to the trial. While Dr. Dembski and seven other proponents of intelligent design signed on as expert witnesses to defend the Dover board, only three of those eight actually appeared in court—and Dembski was not among them. Citing conflicts of interest with their publishers and demanding personal counsel during their depositions (in addition to the lawyers representing the Dover board), one by one most of the experts favoring ID declined to appear in court. Perhaps they knew what was about to transpire.

What did take place in the courtroom was, by any standard, a scientific rout. The key arguments of the ID movement were examined in the trial, and one by one they collapsed, often in spectacular fashion. Claims of "peer review" for an ID book were shown to be not quite what they seemed, and the "research" produced by ID proponents clearly failed to meet any reasonable definition of science. Attorneys for the board, as part of their defense, had promised they would show that ID met the legitimate standards for a scientific theory. To say that they failed in this regard would be almost too kind, and that is the first lesson from the Dover trial.

The Fossil Record

Claims that ID presents a genuine scientific alternative to evolution often begin with the supposed inadequacies of the fossil record and in particular with the claim that the fossil record lacks the "transitional" or "intermediate" forms that would be required to document evolution. If there are no such intermediates, the argument goes, then the fossil record simply does not contain the evidence for evolution that Darwin's enthusiasts pretend.

This charge is demonstrably false, as the National Academy of Sciences has pointed out on several occasions. In reality, although the fossil record is incomplete in many places, there are many important transitions that are richly documented with highly detailed fossil evidence: "So many intermediate forms have been discovered between fish and amphibians, between amphibians and reptiles, between reptiles and mammals, and along the primate lines of descent that it often is difficult to identify categorically when the transition occurs from one to another particular species."[9]

During the trial this point was made brilliantly by Kevin Padian, curator of the Museum of Paleontology at the University of California, Berkeley. Citing a series of specific, well-documented fossil transitions, Padian tore apart contentions that the record of life on earth lacks evidence for evolution. One of his prime examples was the expanding paleontological record of early cetaceans, swimming mammals that today include whales and dolphins. Although the literature of the ID movement, including the textbook *Of Pandas and People,* has claims that the fossil record of these organisms contains no clear intermediate forms between land-dwelling and aquatic animals, Padian calmly summarized the wealth of evidence to the contrary. One of his examples was *Rodhocetus kasrani,* a striking fossil unearthed by a joint American-Pakistani team and reported in the journal *Science* (Figure 2).[10] *Rodhocetus* showed clear evidence of its

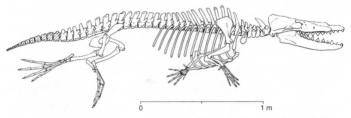

FIGURE 2: Composite restoration of the skeleton of a paddling *Rodhocetus kasrani* to show the morphology of this primitive protocetid. (From Philip D. Gingerich, Munir ul Haq, Intizar H. Khan, and M. Sadiq Malkani, "Origin of Whales from Early Artiodactyls: Hands and Feet of Eocene Protocetidae from Pakistan," *Science* 293 (2002): 2239–42. Used with permission. Illustration: Doug Boyer.) Reprinted with permission from AAAS.

terrestrial origins but included a number of adaptations that suited it well for life in the water. It was, in many ways, exactly the sort of transitional form that the ID movement has claimed could not exist. But there it was.

Several competing teams have now unearthed more than a score of fossil specimens detailing the land-to-water transition that took place in these animals over several million years. The transition is now known in such detail that paleontologist Hans Thewissen felt bold enough to write a review of the discoveries under the title "Whale Origins as a Poster Child for Macroevolution."[11]

One might think that the scientific community, having provided decisive evidence of this evolutionary transition, would now rest on its laurels and allow the reality of this transition to sink in to evolution's critics. But the self-critical nature of the scientific enterprise would not permit this for a second. If these organisms were genuine intermediate forms, then something remarkable must have happened within the skulls of these organisms. The morphology of their hearing organs had to change drastically to accommodate their new lives under water. The highly sensitive hearing mechanisms of modern cetaceans are quite different from the outer and middle ears of land-dwelling mammals. If this fossil series actually contains authentic transitional forms, it should also document the way in which the hearing apparatus was remodeled through intermediate stages to produce a hearing mechanism suited for life under water. A careful study of fossil specimens has now shown that this is indeed the case, including a predicted intermediate form capable of hearing in both air and water.[12] As the authors of this study note: "Sound transmission mechanisms change early on in whale evolution and pass through a stage (in pakicetids) in which hearing in both air and water is unsophisticated. This intermediate stage is soon abandoned and is replaced (in remingtonocetids and protocetids) by a sound transmission mechanism similar to that in modern toothed whales."[13]

The key point should be clear. Even as scientists place these intermediate forms under the microscope, the evidence for evolution is upheld, and the old claim of no intermediate forms rings hollow indeed.

Human Chromosomes

Just two weeks before the Dover ID trial was called to order, our side received what could only be called a gift from God. The journal *Nature* published the chimpanzee genome sequence. The utility of this new information in establishing the validity of evolutionary theory could hardly be understated. As the authors of the lead article on this breakthrough observed: "More than a century ago Darwin and Huxley posited that humans share recent common ancestors with the African great apes. Modern molecular studies have spectacularly confirmed this prediction and have refined the relationships, showing that the common chimpanzee (*Pan troglodytes*) and bonobo (*Pan paniscus* or pygmy chimpanzee) are our closest living evolutionary relatives."[14]

To bring the weight of this evidence into the courtroom, we chose a simple example that provides a direct test of the hypothesis of common ancestry for our species. As any biology student knows, we humans normally have forty-six chromosomes. These chromosomes, which contain nearly all of our genetic information, are arranged in twenty-three pairs—a newborn baby has twenty-three chromosomes from its mother and twenty-three from its father. If we do indeed share common ancestry with the great apes, organisms such as the gorilla, orangutan, and chimpanzee, there's a bit of a problem—all of these great apes have forty-eight chromosomes, arranged in twenty-four pairs. If we really do share a common ancestor with these species, then what happened to that extra pair of chromosomes?

One might make the suggestion that in the lineage leading to our species, a pair of chromosomes simply was lost or discarded. Unfortunately, in genetic terms, that is not a realistic suggestion. There are so many important genes on every primate chromosome that the loss of both members of a chromosome pair would be fatal. The only realistic possibility is that two different primate chromosomes were accidentally fused into one at some point in human evolution. Chromosome fusions of this sort are not at all uncommon and would indeed have reduced the chromosome number from forty-eight to forty-six. But if this sort of fusion did take place in the recent past, it should have left unmistakable evidence behind. Somewhere in the human genome there should be a chromosome still bearing the marks of that fusion, and therein lies an opportunity to put the hypothesis to a scientific test.

What would a fused chromosome look like? The tips of chromosomes, which are called telomeres, contain unique DNA sequences that are easy to recognize. If two chromosomes fused into one, the fusion site would contain telomere DNA sequences where they simply do not belong, on either side of the fusion site. In addition, each chromosome also contains a region known as the centromere where chromosomes attach to the machinery that separates them during cell division. Centromeres also have distinctive DNA sequences that enable them to be easily identified. If one of our chromosomes had indeed been produced by the fusion of two others in the recent past, that chromosome should contain telomere sequences near the middle of the chromosome and should also contain two centromere sequences (see Figure 3).

Now our task gets interesting. We can scan the human genome and see if any of our chromosomes fits this very precise description. If we do not find such a chromosome, then the hypothesis of common ancestry for our species may be disproved, or at least cast into serious doubt. But if we do find a fused chromosome, then a specific evolutionary prediction is fulfilled. So, which is it?

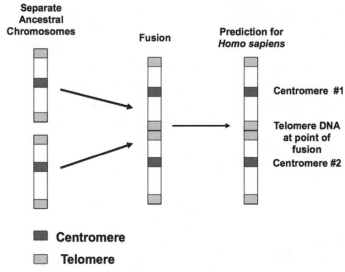

FIGURE 3: The marks of chromosome fusion.

The answer, provided in dramatic detail by the Human Genome Project, is that evolution got it exactly right.[15] The solution is found in human chromosome number 2, which does indeed contain telomere DNA sequences at the fusion point and carries the remnants of two centromere sequences. One of these is still active in humans and corresponds to the centromere for chimp chromosome 12. The other has been inactivated, which makes the fused chromosome more stable during cell division, but it is still recognizable as corresponding to the centromere from chimp chromosome 13. The conclusion from these data is unavoidable—we do indeed share a common ancestor with these species, a common ancestor that possessed, in the recent past, forty-eight chromosomes. No fingerprint left at the scene of a crime was ever more decisive than this genetic evidence. We evolved.

Is there any way these data can be seen as evidence of a de novo creation or "design" of our species without ancestry from another species? The simple answer is "no." The data frankly contradict that conclusion—unless, of course, one is willing to contrive a creator or designer with such a capricious nature that he or she was willing to give us a chromosome number 2 rigged to fool us into believing that we had evolved. The scientific "value" of such an explanation is hardly worth examining.

The judge in the Dover trial listened to exactly this testimony and then waited, no doubt, for some sort of rebuttal or challenge from the other side, the defenders of "intelligent design." That rebuttal never came. Like most of the scientific testimony in the trial, it simply was not questioned by attorneys making the case for ID. Perhaps they feared that making such a challenge would only draw the court's attention to the strength of the scientific case for evolution, and if they ignored such testimony, perhaps the judge would, too. If that was their thinking, it was sorely mistaken.

Smashing the Icons of ID

The crown jewels of the ID movement are a series of examples of "design" to which they claim to have applied the modern tools of biochemistry and molecular biology. These are a number of complex biological systems, including, most famously, the bacterial flagellum, the vertebrate blood-clotting system, and the gene-shuffling mechanism of the immune system. These "icons" of design are examples of systems that supposedly could not have been produced by evolution, and therefore, must have been created from scratch by the actions of a supernatural power—or "designed," in the parlance of the movement.

In making the claim of design, the ID movement has realized, to its credit, that it is liable to fall into the trap of making an "argument from ignorance" by attributing any structure or system whose evolution has not yet been explained to a "designer." In reality, this is an exceptionally weak argument, as even the proponents of design admit. In 1950, for example, one might have observed that no known molecule could account for the special properties of the genetic material, and by inference that supernatural forces must direct inheritance. Just three years later, the double-helix model of DNA structure solved that problem. In 1970 we might have stated that no genetic mechanism existed to account for the incredible diversity of antibody proteins, and therefore the hand of a designer must shape our immune systems. But just six years later Susumu Tonegawa discovered the gene-shuffling system (technically called VDJ recombination) that does exactly that. Or, as we have seen, in 1970 one might also have argued that there were no plausible fossil ancestors for whales and dolphins, and therefore the first appearance of cetaceans on the earth could be attributed to design. Dig up a score of fossil species, and that argument too vanishes into the mists.

What the proponents of ID have done, therefore, is to recast the argument from ignorance in a most interesting way. It is easy enough to point out systems for which we do not as yet have detailed evolutionary explanations—but the assertions of today's ID movement go much further. It claims to have found a reason why the evolution of such complex systems is not possible—even in principle—by evolutionary means. That reason is something known as "irreducible complexity." The principle of "irreducible complexity" is the claim that complex biological systems are composed of multiple parts, and that the removal of just one part would effectively cause the system to stop functioning. If things like the bacterial flagellum or the blood clotting system are irreducibly complex, then they couldn't have evolved a few parts at a time because the intermediate stages would be missing key parts, and they wouldn't work. Without some useful function to give those bits and pieces survival value, natural selection could never drive the pathway leading to the final complex structure, and evolution would fail.

The great discovery of today's intelligent design movement, according to its proponents, is that irreducibly complex systems do exist and that they are vital to life itself. One of these systems, cited so often in the Dover trial that its very mention became a running joke, is the bacterial flagellum. The flagellum is an ion-powered rotary motor that spins a whip-like protein structure at the cell surface to propel bacteria through liquids, almost like an outboard engine on a speedboat. It is indeed a marvelous little machine, and it consists of thirty to forty different proteins (the number varies from species to species) organized to function with remarkable efficiency.

In the case of the flagellum, the assertion of irreducible

complexity means that a minimum number of protein components, perhaps thirty, are required to produce a working flagellum with biological function. By the logic of irreducible complexity, these individual components should have no function until all thirty are put into place, at which point the function of motility appears. The flagellum starts spinning, and it suddenly becomes useful to the cell that possesses it. What this means, according to ID, is that evolution could not have fashioned those components a few parts at a time, since those parts do not have functions that could be favored by natural selection. As ID proponent and Dover witness Michael Behe wrote: "Natural selection can only choose among systems that are already working,"[16] and an irreducibly complex system does not work unless all of its parts are in place. The flagellum is irreducibly complex, and therefore, it must have been designed.

There is just one problem with this argument—the assertion at its very core is dead wrong. That assertion is that useful biological function appears only when each and every part of the system has been put together. Michael Behe has stated this point clearly: "An irreducibly complex system cannot be produced directly by numerous, successive, slight modifications of a precursor system, because any precursor to an irreducibly complex system that is missing a part is by definition nonfunctional."[17] And there's the problem. It turns out that bits and pieces of the bacterial flagellum are indeed functional in a variety of contexts.

An exhaustive analysis along these lines has been done by Mark J. Pallen and Nick Matzke, but one example will suffice to destroy the ID argument.[18] Comparative studies of other bacteria, bacteria which do not contain flagella, show that many of them do possess a structure in their cell membranes resembling a tiny syringe. They use the syringes, which are technically known as Type-III secretion systems (TTSS), to attach to cells of a host organism and then to inject those cells with bacterial poisons. Many of the nastiest bacteria known to science are Type-III secreters, including *Yersinia pestis,* which causes bubonic plague. Incredibly, the proteins making up this nifty little syringe match ten proteins in the base of the bacterial flagellum almost exactly. Clearly, the TTSS by itself does not show how the flagellum evolved, but its very existence demolishes the central claim of the ID movement with regard to irreducible complexity. The core of the ID argument, after all, is that *any precursor to an irreducibly complex system that is missing a part is by definition nonfunctional.* Compared with the flagellum, the TTSS is missing at least twenty parts, and yet it is perfectly functional.

The concept of "irreducible complexity," the very heart and soul of today's ID movement, is built around the claim that bits and pieces of irreducibly complex systems cannot have useful functions of their own. Once one finds exactly such functions (in the TTSS) for a subset of the proteins in ID's favorite icon, the bacterial flagellum, the argument is destroyed. One may, of course, always retreat to the argument from ignorance and point out that evolution has not yet provided a detailed Darwinian pathway to the flagellum. But the special claim of ID to have found a reason why the flagellum is literally un-evolvable has indeed collapsed.

In the Dover courtroom, this collapse took place in

plain sight, for everyone to see. Michael Behe spent three days on the stand of the Harrisburg courtroom attempting to salvage the biochemical argument from design, and he failed. Judge Jones's opinion described this failure in terse, yet telling, language:

> As irreducible complexity is only a negative argument against evolution, it is refutable and accordingly testable, unlike ID, by showing that there are intermediate structures with selectable functions that could have evolved into the allegedly irreducibly complex systems. (2:15–16 (Miller)). Importantly, however, the fact that the negative argument of irreducible complexity is testable does not make testable the argument for ID. (2:15 (Miller); 5:39 (Pennock)). Professor Behe has applied the concept of irreducible complexity to only a few select systems: (1) the bacterial flagellum; (2) the blood-clotting cascade; and (3) the immune system. Contrary to Professor Behe's assertions with respect to these few biochemical systems among the myriad existing in nature, however, Dr. Miller presented evidence, based upon peer-reviewed studies, that they are not in fact irreducibly complex.[19]

Two other systems were mentioned in the court's decision, the blood-clotting cascade and the immune system. Both of these had been invoked as examples of irreducible complexity and therefore as evidence of design, and both collapsed upon inspection. The cascade is an intricate system of more than a dozen proteins that clots vertebrate blood, and ID advocates have routinely stated that it is "irreducibly complex" and stated that each and every one of the proteins in the system must be present or blood does not clot. Clearly a system that fits that description could not have evolved, and therefore it must have been specially created by the designer. Behe himself has written: "Since each step necessarily requires several parts, not only is the entire blood-clotting system irreducibly complex, but so is each step in the pathway.... In the absence of any of the components, blood does not clot, and the system fails."[20]

Once again, the facts betray ID. Biologists have known for more than three decades that the blood of whales and dolphins is, in fact, missing one of the components of the cascade, and yet their blood clots quite well. If one were tempted to dismiss this as a harmless exception to the general rule, a recent study by Yong Jiang and Russell F. Doolittle made that impossible. The blood of the puffer fish is actually missing three of the factors and still has a workable clotting system. Even more significantly, Jiang and Doolittle showed that the major components of the clotting system are actually present in the sea squirt, an invertebrate relative of the organisms from which vertebrates split off more than 400 million years ago.[21] Even though none of the 16,000 genes of the sea squirt codes for anything resembling a vertebrate clotting factor, copies of all but two of the protein domains from which those factors are built are found scattered around its genome. In effect, the sea squirt has nearly all of the nuts and bolts—all of the spare parts—that would have been necessary to piece the first clotting factors together 400 million years ago. In short, the data support evolution, not "design."

The court was treated to a similar story with respect to the immune system, another of the systems that Behe and other ID proponents had claimed to be unevolvable. Behe, in fact, had actually written in *Darwin's Black Box*

that science would never find an evolutionary explanation for the immune system because it was composed
of multiple parts and therefore was irreducibly complex.[22] Fortunately, the scientific community did not take
his advice and vigorously investigated the origins of the
system. As a result, a slew of high-quality scientific papers document the range and depth of this investigation
and lead to the conclusion that the gene-shuffling capa-
bilities of the system did, in fact, evolve from a group
of DNA sequences known as transposons. During the
Dover trial, this evidence was piled in front of Dr. Behe,
and his dismissive attitude made a clear impression upon
the court:

> Between 1996 and 2002, various studies confirmed each ele-
> ment of the evolutionary hypothesis explaining the origin
> of the immune system. (2:31 (Miller)). In fact, on cross-
> examination, Professor Behe was questioned concerning his
> 1996 claim that science would never find an evolutionary
> explanation for the immune system. He was presented with
> fifty-eight peer-reviewed publications, nine books, and sev-
> eral immunology textbook chapters about the evolution of
> the immune system; however, he simply insisted that this
> was still not sufficient evidence of evolution, and that it was
> not "good enough" (23:19 (Behe)).[23]

Judge Jones went on to write that Behe's cavalier dis-
missal of an entire body of research amounted to the
construction of a "scientifically unreasonable burden
of proof" for evolution. And so it was. The scientific
collapse of ID was complete. What was to come was
something even more dramatic—an unmasking of its own
"evolution."

A Rose by Any Other Name

One often hears defenders of ID proudly proclaim that they are "not creationists." When they seem to mean by that is that they are not the sort of "young-earth creationists" who demonstrate allegiance to Genesis by requiring that the earth be no older than 6,000 years. The high point for the young-earth creationist movement in the United States came in the early 1980s when the legislatures of two states, Arkansas and Louisiana, passed laws requiring that "creation science" be taught alongside evolution whenever the subject is broached in public school classrooms. Creation science got a bad name when it was identified as a religious doctrine in the landmark *Edwards v. Aguillard* case, decided by a 7–2 Supreme Court decision in 1987. From that point on, antievolutionists have been careful not to refer to themselves as creationists, even though it is clear that many of them are. Not only would that brand of antievolution be legally suspect, but as they found out in the 1980s, it also places them in conflict with geologists, physicists, and astronomers, as well as the biologists who are their principal targets. No point in biting off more than you can chew and incurring the wrath of the Supreme Court in the process.

No, we are told, the ID movement is something genuinely new, scientific, and logically independent from old-fashioned creationism. A perfect example of this can be found in Stephen C. Meyer's January 28, 2006, op-ed piece in the British paper *The Telegraph,* entitled "Intelligent Design Is Not Creationism." Meyer, who describes himself as "one of the architects of the theory" of intelligent design says that he "knows it isn't" creationism.[24]

Curiously, however, the key documents of the ID movement tell a very different story. When the Dover Board of Education sought to tell its students about ID, they chose an intelligent design textbook known as *Of Pandas and People.*[25] Taking folks like Stephen Meyer at their word, it would seem that this could not be a "creationist" book, since ID is so different from creationism. Yet, once again, a funny thing happened on the way to the trial. Attorneys for the parent plaintiffs subpoenaed the book's publisher for earlier editions of the book, page proofs, editorial copy, and so forth that might help explain how *Pandas* came to be. What they found was a genuine shocker. Paragraph after paragraph of *Pandas* matched up with nearly identical paragraphs of earlier versions of the book and manuscript. But there was a remarkable difference between early and later drafts. Consider this sentence from *Pandas,* explaining the meaning of the term "intelligent design" to students: "*Intelligent design* means that the various forms of life began abruptly through an *intelligent agency,* with their distinctive features already intact—fish with fins and scales, birds with feathers, beaks and wings, etc."[26]

The definition of "intelligent design" certainly sounds scientific, and it doesn't even mention the word "creation." But an earlier version of the text, known as *Biology and Origins,* shows where this paragraph came from: "*Creation* means that various forms of life began abruptly through the agency of an *intelligent creator,* with their distinctive features already intact—fish with fins, birds with feathers, beaks and wings, etc."[27]

This paragraph is but one example of the way in which *Pandas* began its publishing life as an overtly creationist textbook and then morphed into an ID text. How was this transformation accomplished? In most cases, nothing more was required than pasting the word "design" in place of "create" and using the term "designer" instead of "Creator." As Dr. Barbara Forrest of Southeastern Louisiana University demonstrated at the Dover trial, these changes in wording did not occur gradually—they were abrupt. One of Dr. Forrest's demonstratives from the Dover trial showed just how sudden these changes were (see Figure 4).

Clearly something remarkable must have happened in 1987 when the word counts for these two terms literally reversed themselves. What was it? The Supreme Court's judgment in *Edwards v. Aguillard.* Within a few months of the Edwards decision, the publishers of this book decided upon the term "intelligent design," fired up their word processors, and did a global "find and replace." By the simple act of taking a creationist textbook and substituting the term "designer" in place of "Creator," they produced an ID textbook.

Of all the weeks of trial testimony and argument, I am not sure that any piece of evidence ever matched this one for sheer dramatic value. The sudden reversal of these two terms (in Figure 4) sealed the case for anyone who might have been tempted to doubt that ID is not good, old-fashioned American creationism. And as if this was not enough, the three expert witnesses for ID at the Dover trial each admitted, under oath, that ID required the involvement of the supernatural, marking it as a clearly religious idea. One of them, Steven William Fuller, was even candid enough to admit that "it is ID's project to change the ground rules of science to include the supernatural."[28]

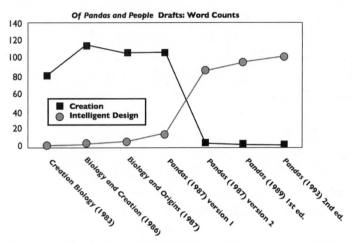

FIGURE 4: Word counts showing the number of cognates of the terms "creation" and "intelligent design" in various editions and drafts of the ID textbook *Of Pandas and People,* published by The Foundation for Thought and Ethics. (Data provided by Dr. Barbara Forrest and used by permission.)

Faced with the creationist history of ID's own textbook and the admission from its own experts that the whole idea of ID is to bring the supernatural into science classrooms, the religious roots of the movement were laid bare for all to see. The game was over, and it was no longer possible to pretend that ID is anything but a renaming of old-fashioned creationism. A rose by any other name might smell as sweet, but creationism renamed is still creationism.

Was God on Trial?

The media attention received by the Dover ID trial lent itself to the temptation of oversimplification. Like similar confrontations, including the 1925 Scopes trial and the 1982 trial on the Arkansas creation science law, it was all too easy to characterize the proceedings as "God vs. Science," and many fell into the trap. Critics of the decision were quick to see it as a blow against religious free expression and an example of the willingness of Darwinist elites to censor competing ideas.

In reality it was none of these things, but the perception of scientific hostility to religion nonetheless lies at the very root of the antievolution movement in the United States. The ID movement not only has taken advantage of this perception but has done everything it can to widen the gulf between people of faith and the scientific community. Indeed, the very choice of the term "intelligent design" has made it easy to argue that those who oppose the movement are antireligious.

Consider, for a moment, what a theist in any sense of the word believes about our universe. To hold to a belief in a supreme being is to see a sense of order, meaning, and purpose in existence. In other words, to see an "intelligent design" to the universe. For what it is worth, that is a view I hold myself.

But that is not what is meant by "intelligent design" in the context of this struggle in the United States. The advocates of "intelligent design" actually propose that the universe is *not* so intelligently designed as to make the evolution of life either possible or inevitable. Rather, they propose that creative, supernatural intervention into the universe was required to bring about the origin of life, the functional design of biochemical systems and pathways, the origins of species, and every major innovation in life's history on this planet. They have no evidence of this, except for a collection of arguments as to why evolution could not accomplish these tasks, and therefore they invoke "design" as the only possible alternate explanation. What they mean by "design," however, is not design itself but rather direct, creative action on the part of their unnamed "designer." They propose what can only be called special creation, since each instance of "design" would require a unique, creative, supernatural act to accomplish what they propose.

In this sense, what is called ID in the United States today is nothing more than old-fashioned scientific creationism, dressed up in the new languages of biochemistry and molecular biology in an attempt to masquerade as a scientific theory. This makes it distinctly different from the more sweeping concepts of meaning, purpose, and design that are part of theistic philosophy and places it squarely in the camp of old-fashioned antievolutionism. The advocates of ID would like to pretend that those who resist it are against belief itself, but what we are really opposing is their attempt to place faith and scientific reason in opposition to each other.

The Champions of Disbelief

It is certainly true that the ID movement has had plenty of help in making the point that evolution can and is being used as a weapon against religious faith. An oft-cited book review written by philosopher David Hull is one of their prime examples: "Whatever the God implied by evolutionary theory and the data of natural history may be like, He is not the Protestant God of waste not, want not. He is also not a living God who cares about his productions. He is not even the awful God portrayed in the book of Job. The God of the Galápagos is careless, wasteful, indifferent, almost diabolical. He is certainly not the sort of God to whom anyone would be inclined to pray."[29]

Hull's point seems to be that God, if He exists, is a pretty nasty fellow. His evidence, naturally enough, is nature red in tooth and claw, a natural world containing an evolutionary process he regards as "rife with happenstance, contingency, incredible waste, death, pain, and horror."[30] No God could allow such horrors, so there can be no God, according to Hull.

The distinguished evolutionary biologist Richard Dawkins has been even more explicit on this point, making it clear that his view of the evolutionary process is at least as bleak as Hull's: "In a universe of blind physical forces and genetic replication, some people are going to get hurt, other people are going to get lucky, and you won't find any rhyme or reason in it, nor any justice. The universe we observe has precisely the properties we should expect if there is, at bottom, no design, no purpose, no evil and no good, nothing but blind pitiless indifference."[31]

Curiously lost in this rush to assert the pointlessness of life is the sense of delight with which Darwin himself approached the evolutionary process—namely, that "from so simple a beginning endless forms most beautiful and most wonderful have been, and are being, evolved."[32] The modern view, it would seem, has wrung the sheer delight out of Darwin's vision and enlisted it in a philosophical assault against religion. Reading such pronouncements, one cannot help but notice how neatly they fit into the strategic plans of the antievolution movement. Indeed, it is by making evolutionary science the enemy of God, according to Phillip Johnson, intellectual godfather of the ID movement, that the religious aims of ID can be realized: "The objective [according to Johnson] is to convince people that Darwinism is inherently atheistic, thus shifting the debate from creationism vs. evolution to the existence of God vs. the non-existence of God. From there people are introduced to 'the truth' of the Bible and then 'the question of sin' and finally 'introduced to Jesus.' "[33]

Considerations such as these led columnist Madeleine Bunting of the *Guardian* to explain to her readers "Why the intelligent design lobby thanks God for Richard Dawkins," noting that "Anti-religious Darwinists are promulgating a false dichotomy between faith and science that gives succour to creationists."[34] Exactly so.

Philosophy and Science

Philosopher Daniel Dennett once characterized natural selection as a process that creates "design out of Chaos without the aid of Mind."[35] One may suppose that it is the business of philosophers to tell us what science means, but there is an inherent danger in that process, and that is the possibility of confusing philosophical pronouncements with actual science. Philosophy may strive to be rigorous and logical, and it may be informed by science, but it is not subject to the empirical tests of science itself. Dennett, of course, used his characterization of natural selection accounting for the presence of order

and "design" without a "mind" for a very specific reason
—to rule out the existence of God.

As an experimental scientist, what I find especially
noteworthy in pronouncements from individuals such as
Hull, Dennett, and Dawkins is an assumption implicit in
their use of evolutionary science in philosophy. That assumption is that science alone can lead us to truth regarding the purpose of existence—which is, of course, that it
does not have one. This may be true, of course, but it is
not a scientific statement because it is not testable by
the methods of science. In fact, David Hull's pronouncements about the "waste" and "horror" of existence have
no more scientific standing than a faith-based assertion
one might make echoing the words of Darwin to describe
the profusion of "endless forms most beautiful and most
wonderful" in the world of life.

In the same way, when Dennett rules out a "Mind" in
nature on the basis of natural selection's ability to create
"design" out of "chaos," he looks only at the direct results of evolution and fails to ask the question of what
makes the process of natural selection possible in the first
place. He would agree, I am certain, that the capacity for
this process is built into the fabric of the natural world, an
inherent part of the physics and chemistry of matter itself. If this is true, then the chaos he so disparages actually contains the seeds to produce, by its own means, the
order, design, and beauty of life in which we so delight.
The ultimate creator and sustainer of that "chaos" would
therefore seem to deserve, one would suspect, a certain
amount of credit. No less credit, to be sure, than the
very designer-God that Dennett is eager to rule out. As a

result, the notion that we live in a universe of meaning and purpose, it seems to me, is validated rather than contradicted by the ever-expanding evolutionary possibilities of existence.

My views on nature of existence do not, of course, amount to scientific statements even if I regard them as being informed by science. Nor, for that matter, do those of the philosophical materialists who would deny a purpose and meaning to our existence. The reason I point this out is to emphasize that a commitment to scientific rationalism does not require a similar commitment to scientific absolutism. To say that the process of science is the only method we have of knowing anything about the natural world is not to claim that science is the only way we have of knowing anything. To do so would be to reduce all forms of human knowledge to empirical science and to impoverish the intellect in its search for knowledge and understanding.

Faith and Science

Those who would argue that science in general and evolutionary science in particular are the enemies of faith are overlooking the distinction between science itself and the philosophical conclusions that one draws from science. For example, one may look at recent new books and find three that directly attack the validity of religion, each of which cite science in so doing. These are *Letter to a Christian Nation* by Sam Harris, *Breaking the Spell* by Daniel Dennett, and *The God Delusion* by Richard Dawkins. Since evolutionary biology occupies a central place in each of these narratives, a conclusion that evolution itself is the enemy of religion is easy to come by. Too easy, to be sure. As a result, people of faith may reflexively attack evolution itself, thinking that they need to invalidate the very core of the biological sciences in order to defend their faith. This is the creationist pathway that the ID movement has taken, and it is a strategy sure to fail.

The proper response requires a recognition that the attacks on religion championed by the three authors mentioned (as well as many others) are built not upon evolution itself. Rather, they depend upon a very specific interpretation of evolution used to justify a materialism that excludes all knowledge outside of science. While this interpretation may be valid, other interpretations are equally valid, including those that see evolution as part of a continuing creative process woven into the fabric of existence. The particular solution for people of faith, therefore, is not to oppose science but to provide an interpretation of science that is in harmony with their religious beliefs. Taking up this task, I am convinced, is the key to making peace between science and religion, a peace that is much to be desired.

I am hardly the first person to make this point. The notion that religion must respect the finding of scientific reason is, in fact, a traditional Western view that has been expressed by many writers in the Abrahamic tradition, none more eloquently than St. Augustine: "Even a non-Christian knows something about the earth, the heavens, . . . the kinds of animals, shrubs, stones, and so forth, and this knowledge he holds to as being certain from reason and experience. Now it is a disgraceful and dangerous thing for an infidel to hear a Christian, presumably giving the meaning of Holy Scripture, talking nonsense on these topics; and we should take all means to prevent such an embarrassing situation, in which people show up vast ignorance in a Christian and laugh it to scorn."[36]

This remarkable passage points out that believers and nonbelievers alike have equal access to observations of the natural world. Therefore, nothing could be worse for people of faith than to defer to the Bible to as a source of scientific knowledge that contradicted direct, empirical studies of nature. Augustine, one of the most prolific and influential of the early Christian writers, got the relationship between scripture and empirical science exactly right. He warned of the danger inherent in using the Bible as a book of geology, astronomy, or biology, admonishing the faithful that to do so would hold the book up to ridicule and disproof. To Augustine, the eternal spiritual truth of the Bible would only be weakened by pretending that it was also a book of science.

What sort of science would we get if we followed Augustinian precepts? That's an excellent question, and one I am quick to answer, especially in front of scientific audiences who might be suspicious of the writings of a fifth-century doctor of the early Church. To understand the kind of science that emerges from the Augustinian tradition, one need only to follow the career of an Austrian priest who spent his life in a religious order founded on the teachings of Augustine. This clergyman was religious enough to rise to the rank of abbot of the Augustinian monastery of St. Thomas in Brünn, Austria (a city now called Brno, in the Czech Republic). At one point in his life he became interested in what today we would identify as a scientific question—how do plants pass their characteristics along from one generation to the next? An interesting question, to be sure. How did this young man approach an answer? Did he pray? Of course. Did he delve into scripture? Almost certainly, since daily readings from the Bible were part of his office. But to answer the scientific question, Father Gregor Mendel, acting in the Augustinian tradition, carried out experiments. His work, as students of biology know, formed the basis of the modern science of genetics. So, what kind of science does one get by following the Augustinian tradition? Excellent science, indeed—you get genetics.

Looking Ahead

For science, I believe that the collapse of "intelligent design," so evident in the Dover trial, carries a clear meaning. That is, that the process of science should be respected. Challenges to evolution—or any other scientific theory—are very much within the scope and tradition of science. If the practitioners of ID actually sought to displace evolution scientifically, they needed only to produce the data to support their case, to carry the fight to the scientific community in a way that would win the battle of evidence in the free marketplace of scientific ideas. Instead, they have consistently rejected that route in favor of cultivating political support and generating public relations activity. They have, in effect, sought an intellectual subsidy from agencies of government by begging for handouts in the form of direct injections of their ideas into textbook, classroom, and curriculum. Scientifically, no idea deserves a place in the classroom that it cannot win for itself on the basis of the evidence, evidence that convinces, no matter how reluctantly, the scientific community. The lesson for science is that organized attempts to subvert the scientific process of debate and peer review can and must be resisted. Not just when they happen to be wrong, as is the case with ID, but because they subvert the very process of science itself.

For people of faith, the failure of the intelligent design movement is hardly the disaster that ID proponents might suggest. It is, rather, a genuine opportunity to come to grips with the science of our times. That science, no question about it, presents genuine challenges to religion, but it also provides religion with an extraordinary opportunity to inform and enlighten the scientific vision of our existence.

As if to illustrate a pathway to such understanding, several months ago one of my scientific friends sent me this passage and asked me to guess its author: "According to the widely accepted scientific account, the universe erupted 15 billion years ago in an explosion called the 'Big Bang' and has been expanding and cooling ever since. . . . In our own solar system and on earth (formed about 4.5 billion years ago), the conditions have been favorable to the emergence of life. While there is little consensus among scientists about how the origin of this first microscopic life is to be explained, there is general agreement among them that the first organism dwelt on this planet about 3.5–4 billion years ago."[37]

The "author" of that brief but straightforward account of scientific natural history was, according to my colleague, Pope Benedict XVI. To be perfectly accurate, he was not exactly the "author," since the passage actually comes from the 2004 report of a committee known as the International Theological Commission, but Joseph Cardinal Ratzinger (now Pope Benedict) did indeed supervise the work of the commission and clearly approved its final form. Significantly, the report goes on to make specific comments about evolution that clearly relate to the evolution–ID struggle in the United States: "Many neo-Darwinian scientists, as well as some of their critics, have concluded that, if evolution is a radically contingent materialistic process driven by natural selection and random genetic variation, then there can be no place in it for divine providential causality.... But it is important to note that, according to the Catholic understanding of divine causality, true contingency in the created order is not incompatible with a purposeful divine providence. Divine causality and created causality radically differ in kind and not only in degree. Thus, even the outcome of a truly contingent natural process can nonetheless fall within God's providential plan for creation."[38]

Evolution is indeed a "truly contingent natural process," and the commission's clear statement that such a process can fall within the sphere of divine causality is nothing more than a reaffirmation of the teachings of Aquinas and other Christian writers on divine and natural causality. This kind of clarity, unfortunately, is remarkably rare in public statements on both sides of the religion and science debate today.

Ultimately, the religion and science debate continues because of a deep antagonism between extremists on both sides of the issue. The solution is not to split the difference but to come to a genuine understanding and appreciation of the true depth of scientific and religious thought on the issues at hand. In the specific case of evolution, the sophistication of theological thinking on natural processes and divine will is routinely underestimated by those who would use science as a weapon against faith. Conversely, the religious community often fails to appreciate the self-critical nature of science and the clear recognition of most scientists as to the limitations of scientific inquiry. In the final analysis, both sides may come to realize, as Charles Darwin did, that there is indeed beauty, wonder, and even grandeur in the evolutionary view of life.

Science and Religion
Why Does the Debate Continue?

ALVIN PLANTINGA

First, *is* there a debate? Well yes, I suppose there is. Many Christians have the vague impression that science is somehow unfriendly to religious belief; for other Christians it is less a vague impression than a settled conviction. Similarly, many scientists and science enthusiasts argue that there is opposition between serious religious belief and science; indeed, some claim that religious belief constitutes a clear and present danger to science.[1] Still others see religious belief as steadily dwindling in the face of scientific advance. Our question is: Why does this debate continue?

I shall try to answer that question; more modestly, I shall try to make a contribution to an answer. This debate displays several different loci or topics. (1) There is the association of science with *secularism* or the so-called scientific worldview.[2] (2) There is alleged conflict between scientific theories of evolution and essential aspects of Christianity and other theistic religions—for example, that human beings are created in the image of God. (3) There is alleged conflict between science and the claim, common to theistic religions, that God *acts specially* in the world. Miracles would be one example of special divine action, but there are others as well: for example, Calvin's "Internal Witness of the Holy Spirit" and Aquinas's "Internal Instigation of the Holy Spirit." (4) There is conflict between religious claims and many explanations in evolutionary psychology of such human phenomena as love, altruism, morality, and religion itself. (5) There is conflict between certain classical Christian doctrines—the resurrection of Jesus, for example—and certain varieties of scientific or historical biblical criticism. Finally, (6) there is alleged conflict between the *epistemic attitudes* of science and religion. The scientific attitude, so it is said, involves forming belief on the basis of empirical investigation, holding belief tentatively, constantly testing belief, and looking for a better alternative; the religious attitude involves believing on faith. Clearly I can not address all six of these topics of debate here; I shall confine myself to the first two.

Science and Secularism

Science is often thought to endorse, promote, enforce, imply, or require *secularism;* but what exactly, or even approximately, *is* secularism? Suppose we start with the adjective and sneak up gradually on the noun. According to my dictionary the term "secular" means "of or relating to the worldly or the temporal as distinguished from the spiritual or eternal: not sacred." Here "eternal" would not refer to propositions, properties, numbers, and other abstract objects, which could be thought of as eternal; perhaps we could replace "eternal," here, with "supernatural." On this account, raking your lawn could be secular; praying or worshipping would not. How about secular*ism*? This would be an attitude or a position of some sort: perhaps the position, with respect to some particular area of life, that secular approaches are all that is necessary or desirable in that area of life; no reference to the spiritual or supernatural is needed for proper prosecution of the activities or projects in that area. One might thus embrace secularism with respect to raking the lawn or getting your car repaired: no reference to the supernatural or spiritual is necessary. This is secularism *with respect to x,* for some department or aspect of life *x;* but then what is secularism *tout court?* For present purposes, that would be the idea that a secular approach to *all* of life is satisfactory or required; there is no department or aspect of life where there needs to be, or ought to be, a reference to the supernatural or spiritual. Secularism, so construed, has been an increasing feature of much of Western life, in particular of Western academic and intellectual life, for the past couple of centuries.

There are two basic and vastly different versions of secularism present in contemporary Western academia. One is limned and examined (and rejected) by Bas van Fraassen in his absorbing book *The Empirical Stance,* initially given as lectures in the very series we are celebrating.[3] This variety is intimately connected with science and can be briefly if imprecisely described as the thought that scientific inquiry, or more accurately what van Fraassen calls "objectifying inquiry," is enough. Perhaps a bit more accurately, but still requiring nuance and qualification, it is the position that the broadly scientific picture of the world is enough. Enough for what? Enough for understanding, and enough for practice. Enough as a guide to life, and enough for rightly fixing opinion. This scientific worldview encompasses all we need to know and indeed all we *can* know about our world and about ourselves; if there is anything beyond or in addition to what science (present or future) reveals, it is something with which we neither have nor can have contact.

This variety of secularism is our main focus, but it is important to see that there is another and wholly different species of the same genus. And just as the first, scientific, variety is outlined in van Fraassen's book, so the second, nonscientific variety is sketched in a review of van Fraassen's book by Richard Rorty.[4] As Rorty points out, there is a kind of secularism that pays little attention to science, or at any rate sees its value as merely utilitarian. Rorty may or may not be right about the nature of the practical goals endorsed by this version of secularism; I shall comment instead on its intellectual or perhaps ideological side. Here what is fundamental is a turning away from science and objectifying inquiry, rejecting that whole endeavor as a failed project. And instead of seeing human beings as trying to achieve the truth about our world, it would instead see us, at some deep level, as *constructing* or, better, *constituting* the truth about the world. This way of thinking goes back, of course, to Kant and perhaps indeed to the ancient world, to the Protagorean claim that "man is the measure of all things." Here the fundamental idea is that we human beings, in some deep and important way, are ourselves responsible for the structure and nature of the world—either individually or communally. At this point, naturally, I would like to talk about Kant, but I do not have the space.

Another version of fundamentally the same idea is the claim that there really is not any such thing as truth (with a capital "T," as they like to put it); what there are instead are various substitutes. Sticking with Rorty, for example, there is truth (now with a small "t") as "what our peers will let us get away with saying."[5] This kind of secularism, like scientific secularism, embraces the idea that we have no need to resort to the spiritual or supernatural; we human beings are autonomous and must make our own way, must fashion our own salvation. We are responsible for ourselves, and indeed (as Rorty says) can redefine, remake ourselves. This lust for human autonomy can assume truly heroic proportions, as (if Rorty's account is accurate) with Heidegger's standing appalled at the thought that he was not his own creation, and his remarkable idea that he was *guilty* by virtue of existing in a universe he had not himself created.[6] (Talk about moral scruples and a tender conscience!) The contrast between these two forms of secularism is enormously fascinating. From a Christian perspective the one vastly overestimates us, tending to see us, we ourselves, as the real creators of the world, or at least the real source of its structure; the other vastly underestimates us, tending to see us as just another animal with a peculiar way of making a living.

But our present concern is with scientific secularism.

Let us look a bit further. According to van Fraassen, the development of modern science involves what he calls, perhaps following Rudolf Bultmann, "objectifying inquiry." Objectifying inquiry, he says, is neither necessary nor sufficient for science; nevertheless, he says, it is a prominent and profoundly important feature of most scientific investigation. There are several aspects to this kind of inquiry, but a number of them can be subsumed under the striking phrase "getting ourselves out of the picture."[7] There is getting ourselves *individually* out of the picture: my own likes and dislikes, my own hopes and fears and loves are not to enter into what I do or say as a scientist, although of course they may serve as motivation for engaging in science in the first place or for pursuing one scientific project as opposed to another. The surgeon who dispassionately cuts into another human being displays this kind of objectivity; to achieve it, surgeons ordinarily refuse to operate on family members. Similarly, my own private and idiosyncratic moral judgments are not to enter in, either into my reports of the data, or my theories. Objectivity in this sense is a matter of ignoring or bracketing what pertains to one or some individual(s) as opposed to others.

But science, notoriously, is also said to refrain from moral judgments more generally—not just those that don't enjoy universal assent. And the same goes for likes and dislikes. So there is a stronger sense of objectivity also operative here: stepping away from, bracketing at least some aspects or characteristics of human subjectivity more generally, hoping in this way to achieve objectivity in the sense of faithfulness to the object of inquiry. There is our nearly inevitable propensity for making

moral judgments; objectivity requires that in doing science we see this as something "from our side" as it were,
not to be found in the things themselves (at least for the
purposes of science). Similarly for *teleology:* human subjects display a nearly ineluctable tendency to think in
terms of teleology, perhaps because of our inveterate
practical bent. Another part of objectifying inquiry,
therefore, another part of "taking ourselves out of the
picture" is to think of the world, at least as scientific
object, as involving no purposes, no teleology. This
thought goes all the way back to Francis Bacon:

> Although the most general principles in nature ought to be
> held merely positive, as they are discovered, and cannot with
> truth be referred to a cause; nevertheless the human under-
> standing being unable to rest still seeks something prior in the
> order of nature. And then it is that in struggling towards that
> which is further off it falls back upon that which is more nigh
> at hand; namely, on final causes: which have relation clearly
> to the nature of man rather than to the nature of the universe;
> and from this source have strangely defiled philosophy.[8]

Still further: human beings display a powerful inclina-
tion to *personify* the world: to see it as populated by living
spirits who, like us, love and hate, think, believe, and
reason; for the animist the whole world is alive, perme-
ated by living spirits.[9] And a very special case of this—a
limiting case, as we might think—is our human tendency
to think of the world itself as created and governed by just
one transcendent spirit; theism can thus be thought of as a
limiting case of animism. Now part of taking ourselves
out of the picture is rejecting, at least for scientific purposes, this tendency to personify the world. And if we do

think of theism as a limiting case of animism, then this taking ourselves out of the picture can be seen as a source of *methodological naturalism* (MN).[10]

MN is widely proposed as a constraint on proper science, and indeed it seems to characterize most if not all of contemporary science. MN is not to be confused with *philosophical* or *ontological* naturalism, according to which there is no such person as God or any other supernatural beings. The partisan of MN does not necessarily subscribe to ontological naturalism. MN is a proposed condition on proper science, not a statement about the nature of the universe. (Of course if philosophical naturalism were true, and if we thought of science as an effort to find the truth about our world, then MN would presumably be the sensible way to proceed in science.) The rough and basic idea of MN is that science should be done *as if*, in some sense, ontological naturalism were true; as Hugo Grotius put it, we should proceed as if God is not given. According to MN, therefore, a proper scientific theory can not refer to God or other supernatural agents such as angels or devils or Satan and his cohorts. Further, scientific description or presentation of the data relevant to a given inquiry can not be in terms or categories involving the supernatural. Still further, a scientific theory can not employ what one knows or thinks one knows by way of divine revelation. There will be more to MN than this: for example, it will also involve a constraint on the appropriate body of background knowledge or belief with respect to which a scientific discipline is to be conducted: that background information, presumably, will contain no propositions obviously entailing the existence of God (or other supernatural beings).[11]

I shall say more about MN later; for the moment, we may note that it can nicely be seen as secularism with respect to science. The claim is that science, that striking and important human activity or form of life, has no need of the supernatural or spiritual for its proper prosecution and indeed is best done by deleting any such references. Note the vast difference between *secularism with respect to science* and *scientific secularism.* The former is the claim that *science* can or should proceed without reference to the supernatural; it says nothing about the rest of life. The latter is a variety of secularism *tout court;* it is the claim that *all* of life can or should proceed without reference to the supernatural, because objectifying inquiry is enough for practice as well as for understanding. And now we can note one source of the continuing debate or mistrust between science and religion. Secularism *tout court,* of course, is the enemy of religion; it is the declaration that there is no department or aspect of life where there needs to be, or ought to be, a reference to the supernatural or spiritual. But the religious attitude toward life just is the attitude that the most important project in human life is getting into the right relation with the supernatural. Specified to Christianity, the religious attitude is that the final good, the *summum bonum* for human beings, is to get into the right relationship with God, which is made possible by the incarnation and atonement of the divine son of God. From that perspective, secularism is a maximally mistaken attitude; it is about as far from right as you can get. And the same will go, then, for *scientific* secularism, the variety of secularism according to which objectifying inquiry, the kind of inquiry characteristic of science, is enough for understanding and practice. According to

Christian belief, objectifying inquiry, inquiry characterized by getting ourselves out of the picture, is not anywhere near enough either for theoretical understanding or for knowing how to live a good life. To say it is woefully inadequate would be a colossal understatement.

It is crucially important to see that science itself does not support or endorse scientific secularism or the scientific world picture. Science is one thing; the claim that it is *enough* is a wholly different thing. It is not part of science to make that claim. One will not find it in textbooks of science as such, whether physics, chemistry, biology, or whatever. There are scientists who make this claim; but there are as many who reject it. One can be wholly enthusiastic about science without thinking objectifying inquiry is enough. Indeed, that is the sensible attitude toward science from a Christian perspective. The confusion of science with scientific secularism is egregious; it is little better than confusing, say, music history with the claim that music history is enough, philately with the claim that philately is enough. But I believe this confusion, colossal as it is, is widely perpetrated, and by people from both sides of the divide between science and religion. There are many who enthusiastically endorse science, but they go on to confuse it with scientific secularism. Perhaps this is because they see secularism with respect to science—that is, methodological naturalism, as essential to science—but then confuse it with secularism *simpliciter*. Others who emphatically reject secularism fall into the same confusion. They are suspicious, distrustful of science, because of its association with scientific secularism or the so-called scientific worldview. But the fact that science is associated with secularism—that is, the fact that some people associate the two—is not a decent reason for suspicion of science; it is no better than being suspicious of music history just because someone thinks that it is enough. This confusion, I believe, is one factor underlying the continuing mutual distrust between science and religion. So one factor here is really no more than a confusion.

Evolution

In Galileo's time, so they say, the main source of conflict between science and religion was astronomical; at present it is biological.[12] Ever since Darwin's day, there has been friction, misunderstanding, and mutual recrimination between those who accept Darwinism in one form or another and Christians of various kinds, and of course this conflict is a main source of the continuing debate between religion and science. Many Christian fundamentalists find incompatibility between the contemporary Darwinian evolutionary account of our origins and their version of the Christian faith. Many Darwinian fundamentalists (as the late Stephen Jay Gould called them) second that motion: they too claim there is conflict between Darwinian evolution and classical Christian or even theistic belief. Contemporaries who champion this conflict view would include, for example, Richard Dawkins, Daniel Dennett, and, far to the opposite side, Phillip Johnson.[13] In Darwin's own day, this opposition and strife could assume massive proportions. Now Darwin himself was a shy, retiring sort; he hated public controversy and confrontation, but given what he had to say, he was often embroiled in controversy. Fortunately for him, there was his friend Thomas H. Huxley, who defended Darwin with such fierce tenacity that he came to be called "Darwin's bulldog." Huxley himself continued the canine allusion by referring to some of Darwin's opponents as "curs which will bark and yelp."[14] This canine connection has proved resilient, or at least durable, extending all the way to the present, where we have Richard Dawkins described as "Darwin's Rottweiler," and Daniel Dennett described, unkindly, by the late Stephen Jay Gould, as "Dawkins's lapdog."

Now where, exactly, does conflict or alleged conflict arise? Evolution, of course, is manifold and various; the term covers a multitude—not necessarily a multitude of sins, but a multitude nevertheless. There is (1) the *Ancient Earth Thesis*, the proposition that the earth is billions of years old. (2) There is the proposition that life has progressed from relatively simple to relatively complex forms. In the beginning there was relatively simple unicellular life, perhaps of the sort represented by bacteria and blue-green algae, or perhaps still simpler unknown forms of life. (Although bacteria are simple compared with some other living beings, they are in fact enormously complex creatures.) Then more complex unicellular life, then relatively simple multicellular life such as seagoing worms, coral, and jellyfish, then fish, then amphibia, then reptiles, birds, mammals, and finally, as the culmination of the whole process, and the crown of creation, human beings: the *Progress Thesis*, as we humans like to call it (jellyfish might have a different view as to where the whole process culminates). (3) There is the thesis of *Descent with Modification:* the enormous diversity of the contemporary living world has come about by way of offspring differing, ordinarily in small and subtle ways, from their parents. Connected with the thesis of descent with modification is the (4) *Common Ancestry Thesis:* that life originated just once on earth, all subsequent life being related by descent to those original living creatures—the proposition that, as Gould put it, there is a "tree of evolutionary descent linking all organisms by ties of genealogy."[15] According to the Common Ancestry Thesis, we are all cousins of each other—and indeed of all living things.[16] You and the summer squash in your garden, for example—are really cousins under the skin (rind).

Fifth, there is the claim that a certain particular mechanism drives this process of descent with modification: the most popular candidate is natural selection culling or winnowing random genetic mutation. Since Darwin made a similar proposal ("Natural selection has been the main but not exclusive means of modification"), call this thesis *Darwinism.* Finally, it is often assumed that (6) life itself developed from nonliving matter without any special creative activity of God but just by virtue of processes described by the ordinary laws of physics and chemistry: call this the *Naturalistic Origins Thesis.* These six theses are of course importantly different from each other. They are also logically independent in pairs, except for the third and fifth theses: the fifth entails the third, in that you can not sensibly propose a mechanism for a process without supposing that the process has indeed occurred. Suppose we use the term "evolution" to denote the first four of these; the fifth thesis points to the mechanism allegedly *underlying* evolution, and the sixth is not really part of the theory of evolution.

So where does real or apparent conflict arise? Many Christian evangelicals or fundamentalists accept a literal interpretation of the creation account in the first two chapters of Genesis; they are inclined therefore to think the earth and indeed the universe vastly younger than the billions of years of age attributed to them by current science. This seems to be a fairly straightforward conflict, and hence part of the answer to our question is that current scientific estimates of the age of the earth and of the universe differ widely (not to say wildly) from scripturally based beliefs on the part of some Christians and other theists (Muslims, for example). The ranks of young-earth creationists may be thinning; they are being succeeded by adherents of "intelligent design," who ordinarily hold neither that the earth is young nor that God has directly created representatives of most lineages in more or less their present forms.

A more important source of conflict has to do with the Christian doctrine of creation, in particular the claim that God has created human beings *in his image*. This requires that God *intended* to create creatures of a certain kind—rational creatures with a moral sense and the capacity to know and love him—and then acted in such a way as to accomplish this intention. It does not require that God *directly* create human beings, or that he did not do so by way of an evolutionary process, or even that he intended to create precisely human beings, precisely our species. (Maybe all he actually intended to create were rational, moral, and religious creatures; he may have been indifferent to the specific form such creatures would take.) But if he created human beings in his image, then at the least he intended that creatures of a certain sort come to be, and acted in such a way as to guarantee the existence of such creatures. This claim is consistent with the ancient earth thesis, the progress thesis, the descent with modification thesis, and the common ancestry thesis. It is important to see that it is also consistent with Darwinism. It could be, for example, that God directs and orchestrates the Darwinian process; perhaps, indeed, God causes the right genetic mutation to arise at the right time. There is nothing in the scientific theory of evolution to preclude God from causing the relevant genetic mutations.

What is *not* consistent with Christian belief, however, is the claim that this process of evolution is *unguided*— that neither God nor anyone else has had a hand in guiding, directing, orchestrating, or shaping it. But precisely this claim is made by a large number of contemporary scientists and philosophers who write on this topic. There is a veritable choir of extremely distinguished experts insisting that this process is unguided, and indeed insisting that it is part of contemporary evolutionary theory to assert that it is unguided. Examples would be Stephen Jay Gould, Douglas Futuyma, G. G. Simpson, and many others, but the loudest voices in the choir (the soloists, perhaps) are Richard Dawkins and Daniel Dennett.[17]

One of Dawkins's most influential books is entitled *The Blind Watchmaker*. Its thesis is that the enormous variety of the living world has been produced by natural selection unguided by the hand of God or any other person:

All appearances to the contrary, the only watchmaker in nature is the blind forces of physics, albeit deployed in a very special way. A true watchmaker has foresight: he designs his cogs and springs, and plans their interconnections, with a future purpose in his mind's eye. Natural selection, the blind, unconscious automatic process which Darwin discovered, and which we now know is the explanation for the existence and apparently purposeful form of all life, has no purpose in mind. It has no mind and no mind's eye. It does not plan for the future. It has no vision, no foresight, no sight at all. If it can be said to play the role of watchmaker in nature, it is the *blind* watchmaker.[18]

This thought is trumpeted by the subtitle of the book: "Why the Evidence of Evolution Reveals a Universe Without Design." Why does Dawkins think natural selection is blind and unguided? Why does he think that "the Evidence of Evolution Reveals a Universe Without Design"? How does the evidence of evolution reveal such a thing? What Dawkins does in his book, fundamentally, is three things. First, he nicely recounts some of the fascinating anatomical details of certain living creatures and their ways (bats, for example). Second, he tries to refute arguments for the conclusion that blind, unguided evolution could not have produced certain of the wonders of the living world—the mammalian eye, or the wing. Third, he makes suggestions as to how these and other organic systems could have developed by unguided evolution.

His refutations of these objections are not always successful; what is most striking, however, is the general form of his argument for the conclusion that the universe is without design. His detailed arguments are all for the conclusion that it is *biologically possible* that these various organs and systems should have come to be by unguided Darwinian mechanisms, where he takes it that an outcome is biologically possible if it is not *prohibitively im-*

probable. Of course there are problems with measuring probability here, with saying what degree of improbability is acceptable, and the like. What is truly remarkable, however, is the form of the main argument. The premise he argues for is something like: (1) We know of no irrefutable objections to its being biologically possible that all of life has come to be by way of unguided Darwinian processes; the conclusion is (2) All of life has come to be by way of unguided Darwinian processes.

It is worth meditating, if only for a moment, on the striking distance here between premise and conclusion. The premise tells us, substantially, that for all we know it is possible that unguided evolution has produced all of the wonders of the living world; the conclusion is that unguided evolution has indeed produced all of those wonders. The argument form seems to be something like *there are no irrefutable objections to the possibility of p; therefore p.* Many widely endorsed philosophical arguments are invalid; few display the truly colossal distance between premise and conclusion flaunted by this one. I come home and announce to my wife that I have just been given a $50,000 raise; naturally she wants to know my reason for thinking so; I tell her that no irrefutable objections to its possibility have so far been produced. The reaction would not be pretty. Now perhaps Dawkins has some other unexpressed premises in mind, and perhaps if we added those premises, the argument would be less unimpressive; but would it not be good if he told us what those premises are?

Dawkins utterly fails to show that "the facts of evolution reveal a universe without design"; at best he argues that we do not know that it is astronomically improbable

that the living world is without design. Still, the fact that
he and others assert his subtitle loudly and slowly, as it
were, can be expected to convince many, in particular
those with no particular expertise in the subject, that the
biological theory of evolution is in fact incompatible with
the Christian belief that the living world has been designed. Another source of the continuing debate, therefore, is the mistaken claim on the part of such writers as
Dawkins that the scientific theory implies that the living
world and human beings in particular have not been designed and created by God.

A second prominent authority on the subject is Daniel Dennett; his views are similar to those of Dawkins
(which may be why Gould called him "Dawkins's lapdog"). Dennett's main contribution to the subject is entitled *Darwin's Dangerous Idea*; what is Darwin's idea
and why is it dangerous?[19] In brief, Darwin's idea, an idea
Dennett of course endorses and defends, is the thought
that the living world with all of its beauty and wonder, all
of its marvelous and apparent ingenious design, was not
created or designed by God or anything at all like God;
instead it was produced by natural selection, a blind, unconscious, mechanical, algorithmic process—a process, he
says, that creates "design out of chaos without the aid of
Mind."[20] The whole process has happened without divine
aid. It all happened just by the grace of mindless natural
selection: "An impersonal, unreflective, robotic, mindless
little scrap of molecular machinery is the ultimate basis of
all the agency, and hence meaning, and hence consciousness, in the universe."[21] The idea is that mind, intelligence,
foresight, planning, design are all latecomers in the universe, themselves created by the mindless process of natu-

ral selection. Human beings, of course, are among the products of this mindless process; they are not designed or planned for by God or anyone else. "Here, then, is Darwin's dangerous idea: the algorithmic level *is* the level that best accounts for the speed of the antelope, the wing of the eagle, the shape of the orchid, the diversity of species, and all the other occasions for wonder in the world of nature";[22] in his recent book *Breaking the Spell: Religion as a Natural Phenomenon* he adds that the same goes for the moral sense we humans display, as well as our religious sensibilities, our artistic strivings, and our interest in and ability to do science and mathematics or compose great music or poetry.

Now why is Darwin's idea dangerous? Because if we accept it, thinks Dennett, we are forced to reconsider all our childhood and childish ideas about God, morality, value, the meaning of life, and so on. Theists, naturally enough, believe that God has always existed; so mind has always existed and was involved in the production and planning of whatever else there is. In fact many have thought it *impossible* that mind should be produced just from unthinking matter; as John Locke puts it, "It is as impossible to conceive that ever pure incogitative Matter should produce a thinking intelligent Being, as that nothing should of itself produce Matter."[23] Darwin's idea is that this notion is not merely not impossible; it is the sober truth of the matter. This idea, then, is inconsistent with any form of theism, and Dennett sees serious religion as steadily dwindling with the progress of science. And just as we preserve in zoos animals threatened with extinction, Dennett thoughtfully suggests that we keep a few Baptists and other fundamentalists in something like "cultural zoos" (no doubt with sizable moats to protect the rest of us right-thinking nonfundamentalists). We should preserve a few Baptists for the sake of posterity— but not, he says, at just any cost. "Save the Baptists," says he, "but not *by all means* [Dennett's emphasis]. Not if it means tolerating the deliberate misinforming of children about the natural world."[24] Save the Baptists, all right, but only if they promise not to misinform their children by teaching them "that 'Man' is not a product of evolution by natural selection"[25] and other blatantly objectionable views.[26]

Darwin's idea is incompatible with theism (and most varieties of religion). Of course this doesn't automatically make it *dangerous* to theism—theists might just note the inconsistency and reject it. Many propositions are inconsistent with theism (e.g., *nothing but turtles exist*), but not a danger to it. This idea is dangerous to theism only if it is *attractive,* only if there are good reasons for adopting it and rejecting theism. Why does Dennett think we should *accept* Darwin's dangerous idea? Concede that it is audacious, with it, revolutionary, anti-medieval, quintessentially contemporary, and appropriately reverential toward science, and it has that nobly stoical hair-shirt quality Bertrand Russell said he liked in his beliefs: still, why should we believe it? First, Dennett seems to think Darwin's idea is just part of current biology—that the contemporary neo-Darwinian theory of evolution just is a theory according to which the living world in all its beauty and diversity has come to be by unguided natural selection. That is Darwin's idea, and that idea, he thinks, is a solid part of contemporary biology. But what does he think is the *evidence* for this idea?

Here Dennett follows the same route as Dawkins. He claims that it is *possible* that all the variety of the biosphere be produced by mindless natural selection: "The theory of natural selection shows how every feature of the world *can* be the product of a blind, unforesightful, nonteleological, ultimately mechanical process of differential reproduction over long periods of time."[27] Now clearly the theory of natural selection does not show this at all. Dennett quotes John Locke as holding it impossible that "pure incogitative Matter should produce a thinking intelligent Being"; Locke believed it impossible in the broadly logical sense that mind should have arisen apart from the activity of mind. Supposing, as he did, that matter and mind exhaust the possibilities for concrete beings, he believed that there are no possible worlds in which there are minds at a given time, but no minds at any earlier time; minds can have been produced only by minds. Or by Mind; Locke and other theists will agree that mind is a primitive feature of the universe. God has always existed, never comes into existence, and exists necessarily; at any time *t*, God is present at *t*. The scientific theory of natural selection certainly has not shown that Locke is wrong: it has not shown that it is possible, in the broadly logical sense, that mind arise from "pure incogitative Matter." It does not so much as address that question. But set aside such metaphysical qualms for the moment. What does the theory show, then? It gives us detailed and empirically informed stories—or perhaps a recipe for such stories about how various features of the living world could have come to be by way of natural selection winnowing genetic mutation.[28] Could have come to be in what sense of "could"? Perhaps the thing to say is that these stories are successful if they are reasonably probable—where of course there is ineliminable vagueness; one can not say just how probable a theory must be in order to be *reasonably* probable.

The important point to see is that Dennett just identifies Darwin's idea—that is, the idea that the living world has been produced by a process of unguided natural selection—with the deliverances of contemporary biological science. But how can that be right? True: there is no canonical source telling us exactly and precisely what the contemporary neo-Darwinian theory of evolution comprises. But does it include not merely the idea that the living world has been produced by a process in which natural selection is the chief mechanism, but the vastly more ambitious idea that this process has been unsupervised, unplanned, unintended by God or any other intelligent agent? That hardly seems to be an appropriate part of an empirical scientific theory. It looks instead like a metaphysical or theological add-on. Dennett himself is of course a naturalist; he just adds naturalism to the scientific theory, shakes well, and declares the result part of current science, thus confusing natural selection with *unguided* natural selection.

Here we have another important source of the continuing debate between science and religion. Dawkins and Dennett both hold that contemporary evolutionary theory—Darwinism, in particular—is incompatible with the Christian and theistic claim that God has created human beings in his own image. Both claim that Darwinism, the theory that the principal mechanism driving the process of evolution is natural selection winnowing random genetic mutation, implies that the universe—the living universe, anyway—is without design. Dennett does so simply by identifying current evolutionary theory with the result of annexing to it the proposition that evolution is unguided; Dawkins does so by arguing—ineptly, as we have seen—that Darwinism implies that proposition.

This confusion or alleged connection between Darwinism and unguided Darwinism is perhaps the most important source of continuing conflict and debate between science and religion. According to theistic religion, God has created human beings in his own image. According to current evolutionary theory—Darwinism, anyway—the main mechanism driving the process of evolution is natural selection culling random genetic mutation. So far there is no conflict. God could shape, supervise, direct this process, for example, by protecting certain populations from extinction, arranging for their having a sufficient food supply, and so on. He could be more intimately involved; he could cause the genetic mutations, and cause the right mutations to arise at the right times. But when Dennett, Dawkins, and their friends go on to add that the process is unguided by God or any other intelligent agent, then, of course, conflict and inconsistency arise. Hence if you confuse Darwinism with unguided Darwinism, a confusion Dennett makes and Dawkins encourages, you will see science and religion as in conflict at this point.[29]

There are many manifestations of this confusion. Consider the conflict raging over intelligent design. Here both friends and foes as well as some judges and other allegedly neutral arbiters claim that ID is *incompatible* with evolution. Some of its friends propose that ID be taught as an *alternative* to evolution; foes, naturally, reject that proposal. Both claim that ID is inconsistent with evolution. Now the central claim of ID is that certain organisms or organic systems cannot be explained by unguided natural selection and that the best scientific hypothesis, with respect to those phenomena, is that they have been intelligently designed. This claim, that intelligent design in the living world can be empirically detected, is consistent with Darwinism as such; but of course if you confuse Darwinism with *unguided* Darwinism, or evolution with *unguided* evolution, then you will see ID as incompatible with evolution. This confusion of Darwinism with unguided Darwinism is to be found even in official proclamations of such organizations as the National Association of Biology Teachers. Until 1997 that organization stated as part of its official position that "the diversity of life on earth is the outcome of evolution: an unsupervised, impersonal, unpredictable and natural process."

This confusion between Darwinism and unguided Darwinism is a crucial cause of the continuing debate. Darwinism, the scientific theory, is compatible with theism and theistic religion; unguided Darwinism, a consequence of naturalism, is incompatible with theism but is not entailed by the scientific theory. It is instead a metaphysical or theological add-on.

I close with two objections to my assertion that the scientific theory does not entail unguided Darwinism. One of these is of little consequence; the other is more puzzling. To start with the easy one: Darwinism and theism are compatible, so I say, because it could be that God *causes* the random genetic mutations involved. But, says the objector, if those mutations are caused by God, how could they possibly be *random?* Does not randomness imply that they are uncaused, or at least unplanned? Does it not mean that they happen just by chance?

The answer is easy enough: to say that a mutation is random, in the biological sense, is only to say that it does not arise out of the design plan of the creature to which it accrues and is not a response to its adaptational needs. Thus Ernst Mayr, the dean of post–World War II biology: "When it is said that mutation or variation is random, the statement simply means that there is no correlation between the production of new genotypes and the adaptational needs of an organism in the given environment."[30] He adds, "If we say that a particular mutation is random, it does not mean that a mutation at that locus could be anything under the sun, but merely that it is unrelated to any current needs of the organism or is not in any other way predictable."[31] But clearly a mutation could be random in *this* sense and also caused; indeed, caused by God. In this way God could guide and orchestrate the whole course of evolution, and do it by way of causing the right random mutations to arise at the right time, allowing natural selection to do the rest.

Some will object to this suggestion as improperly involving divine action in the world; God should not be thought of as intervening in the world he has created. That is, of course, a theological objection that does not really bear on the question of compatibility. But for those who find this theological objection compelling, there is another possibility worth exploring: frontloading. God could create initial conditions that he knows will issue, given the laws he sets for the world, in the right mutations arising at the right time. There is little real difference between (a) God's decreeing at the beginning that at *t*, such and such will happen, on the one hand, and (b) At *t*, God's decreeing that such and such happen then. Our issue, however, is the question whether Darwinism is compatible with God's creating and designing human beings, and creating them in his own image. Clearly these two are compatible.

I turn now to the second objection. Like Dawkins and Dennett, Alex Pruss holds that current evolutionary theory is incompatible with Christian belief, but his suggestion is both more subtle and more plausible.[32] According to Pruss, the modern neo-Darwinian theory asserts at least two things. It asserts, first, that there is a "full ancestral history" of each population of organisms, and indeed of each individual organism. This would be a proposition specifying the ancestors of the individual in question, going all the way back to its very first ancestor (and here again there will be ineliminable vagueness). According to most contemporary experts, life began in just one place; therefore that first ancestor would also be the first ancestor of all living things. This history would also report which mutations occurred to which ancestors, and which of those mutations (by way of natural selection) came to spread to the rest of the relevant population. (It goes without saying that we do not have access to these ancestral histories.) According to Pruss, the claim that there is such a complete ancestral history for each individual is compatible with theism, as is the claim that no special divine action is required for the mutations or for their spreading to the rest of the population by natural selection.

But evolutionary theory makes a further claim: that

an *explanation* of all the current diversity of life is given
by the assertion that it has come to be by way of natural
selection working on random genetic mutation: "It is the
ambitious claim that evolution provides a true explanation of why such marvelously complex and adapted
animals as horses, pine trees and frogs exist, with complex organs such as equine eyes and human brains, and
why intelligent animals like humans exist, an explanation
whose possibility competes with, and undercuts, Paley-
type teleological arguments."[33] It is *this* claim, the claim
"(E) Darwinism provides a true explanation of all the
variety of life, including the existence of human beings,"
says Pruss, that is incompatible with the theistic claim
that God has created human beings in his own image.

Where, exactly, is the incompatibility? The first thing
to note is that explanations come in a wide variety, and
the term "explanation" is a bit of a weasel word. A para-
digm case of explanation: My car will not start. I take it in
to the garage; the mechanic checks the electrical system,
finds no problem, and finally concludes that the problem is a defective fuel pump. He replaces the fuel pump,
whereupon the car starts properly. The explanation of its
failing to start is that it had a defective fuel pump; that is,
the answer to the question *Why did that car fail to start?*
is *It had a defective fuel pump.* Note that (depending on
just how we understand "defective") it is very unlikely
that a car with a defective fuel pump will start.

The explanation E that Darwinism offers is of a different kind: it is *statistical.* This means, says Pruss, that
the explanation works by showing how the *explanans*
is not unlikely: "It is claimed that some set of mutations and environmental interactions that would lead to

the occurrence of a species containing the 'notable' features . . . is not unlikely."[34] Pruss proposes that this statistical variety of explanation is the sort current scientific evolutionary theory claims to give for the variety of terrestrial life. According to the scientific theory of evolution, therefore, the correct answer to the question *Why is there such a thing as human beings or the human brain, or the equine eye?* is *It is not unlikely that these things have come to be by way of natural selection working on random genetic mutation, starting originally from some very simple unicellular form of life.*

Pruss goes on to say, however, that no theist could accept E—that is, no theist could accept the claim that the presence and activity of these processes is the *explanation* of the existence of humanlike creatures (intelligent animals made in the image of God). That is because the theist accepts another proposition that *undercuts* the explanation proposed in E. This proposition, of course, is that God intended all along to create human beings, or at any rate creatures in his image. Pruss's claim is that if you accept *that* proposition, then you can't also accept E; you can't also accept the evolutionary story *as an explanation*.

By way of analogy: suppose Sam contracts lung cancer. One explanation is that he was a smoker for forty years. But now suppose we learn that an ill-disposed physician injected Sam with a serum that invariably causes lung cancer. Then, we might think, Sam's long-term smoking is no longer an explanation, at least for us; it has been undercut, as an explanation, by our knowledge of that rogue physician's malicious activity. When we knew that Sam was a heavy smoker but did not know about the rogue physician, then the fact that he was a smoker was a probabilistic explanation of his getting lung cancer; once we learn about that malevolent physician, the fact of his smoking is no longer a probabilistic explanation, or indeed an explanation of any kind at all. According to Pruss, therefore, you can not both be a theist and sensibly think natural selection is the explanation of the existence of human or humanlike creatures. Is he right? The question divides itself. First, is he right in claiming that it is part of current science, part of the scientific theory of evolution, to claim that natural selection is indeed the true explanation of the existence of humanlike creatures? As I said earlier, there is no canonical axiomatization of the scientific theory of evolution emblazoned on the walls of the National Academy of Sciences or the American Association for the Advancement of Science. Where do you go to find out precisely what this theory says? How can we tell whether this claim of explanation is or is not part of the scientific theory as such, as opposed to an add-on by those who do not accept theism? That is a hard question, and the answer is far from obvious.

Second, is E, the claim that natural selection is a (statistical) explanation of there being humanlike creatures, really incompatible with theism? Not obviously. Let us concede for purposes of argument that a theist can not sensibly accept E; is that sufficient for the proposition that theism is incompatible with E? Maybe not. As Pruss sees it, a proposition's being an explanation sometimes depends on what else you know: if you know that God intended that there be humanlike creatures, then natural selection will not be, for you, a statistical explanation of their existence; if you do not know that, however, it could be. That Sam is a smoker is a statistical explanation of his coming down with cancer—but it is not an explanation for you if you know about that nefarious physician.

This means that a proposition of the sort in question is an explanation *relative to* some body of background information; P can be an explanation relative to my background information without being an explanation relative to yours. We live in North Dakota; the overnight temperature drops below −40; my car won't start. The proposition that most cars will not start at that temperature may be a probabilistic explanation of that event for me, but not for you; that is because you have more detailed knowledge of the cause of this car's failing to start on this occasion (you know I always buy cheap oil that congeals at −40 and that my car is equipped with an inhibitor that prevents its starting when the oil is congealed). But then strictly speaking, the claim that natural selection is a probabilistic explanation of the variety of life does not make sense, just as it stands; it is like saying that Chicago is to the west of. To get a proper assertion, we need to specify which background information it is with respect to that this proposition is an explanation.

Of course the scientific theory in question does not explicitly say. But it seems sensible to suppose, first, that any scientific inquiry proceeds relative to some array of background information. It seems sensible to suggest, second, that the relevant background information will not include propositions obviously implying the existence of God or other supernatural agents; this would be a consequence of the assumption of methodological naturalism, which, at present anyway, constrains most if not all scientific projects. That means, however, that E is not really incompatible with theism. For E is as it stands incomplete; it is the claim that *the coming to be of human-like creatures by way of natural selection* is not massively improbable with respect to an implicitly but not explicitly specified array of background information. That array, however, whatever precisely it is, is constrained by methodological naturalism and therefore contains no propositions implying the existence of supernatural beings. That (1) is a probabilistic explanation of the variety of life relative to *that* array is surely not inconsistent with theism.

I am therefore inclined to think Pruss has not given us a good reason for thinking theism incompatible with evolutionary theory.

Religion vs. Science?

LAWRENCE M. KRAUSS

"Blind respect for authority is the greatest enemy of truth."

ALBERT EINSTEIN

"Science doesn't make it impossible to believe in God. It just makes it possible not to believe in God."

STEVEN WEINBERG

With the 100th anniversary of the inception of the Terry Lectures in mind, I would like to focus on the long-standing tension between science and religion, epitomized in different contexts by the quotations above from two distinguished physicists, the agnostic Albert Einstein and the atheist Steven Weinberg, and on how this tension currently manifests itself in the public debate regarding so-called intelligent design as a scientific alternative to evolution.

Religion and science are in collision today, as they have been many times throughout human history, or at least as long as science has been pursued separately from religion. Two recent examples come to mind: In 2001 in Afghanistan, the Taliban blew up the monumental Buddha

statues at Bamiyan. They destroyed those mammoth statues because they felt that their religion forbade "false
idols" as manifest in statues reproducing human faces and
bodies. The Taliban had nothing specific against Bud-
dhism; they wanted to destroy all statues. Thankfully
they were not able to, although the destruction of the
Buddhas was a great loss for all of humanity. This destruction was also a clear example of religion in conflict
with science—in this case, archaeology, for which the
statues represented priceless artifacts from the past—and
human knowledge itself, inasmuch as these sculptures
were amazing specimens of antiquity for all humanity to
treasure. What motivated this attack? In a word, fear.

At the same time in this country collisions between
science and religion, also based on fear, were taking place.
For example, former House Majority Leader Tom DeLay
—who has, amazingly, a degree in biology—argued that
the Columbine school shootings happened "because our
school systems teach our children that they are nothing
but glorified apes who have evolutionized out of some
primordial soup of mud."[1] This sentence is in quotation
marks because he placed it in the *Congressional Record*. It
epitomizes how deeply an inappropriate religious fear of
the moral implications of evolutionary biology has pene-
trated many levels of government.

The United States is not just an intensely religious
country. Even some of our secular institutions have a
tradition based on sometimes amusing superstitions. This
was driven home to me, for example, when a friend of
mine came back from London and brought me back a
ten-pound note. If you look at the back, you will see that
there is a picture of Charles Darwin there. If, on the other

hand, you look at the back of the U.S. one-dollar bill, you will see that there is a pyramid with an eye on it! Perhaps this says something about deeply rooted differences in our cultures.[2]

Even when statements made in conflict with scientific knowledge are not based on fear, they are often based on ignorance. For example, public policy regarding intelligent design has been defined by people like George W. Bush. Talking about evolution versus intelligent design, Bush once declared that "both sides ought to be properly taught so people can understand what the debate is about."[3] There is nothing wrong with this statement per se. It would, that is, be acceptable, if there really *were* a scientific debate, which there is not.

The intelligent design conflict unfolds against a background of desperate problems in education. Our public schools are not teaching science effectively.[4] As a society, we should be spending our time and energy trying to teach science better in the classrooms, not worse. In this context, the argument over evolution versus intelligent design is a huge waste of time. Having to focus our energies on this attack on science keeps us from finding better ways to teach how remarkable science is in illuminating various aspects of our universe.

Consider some depressing statistics. In one recent study comparing students from twenty-one countries, U.S. twelfth graders performed far below the international average in math and science.[5] In Japan, 66 percent of undergraduates go into science or engineering. In China, 59 percent do so. In America, only 32 percent of undergraduates choose science or engineering. In a 2001 National Science Foundation (NSF) survey of scientific literacy, 53 percent of American adults were unaware that the last dinosaur died before the first human arose. Just 50 percent of American adults knew that the earth orbits the sun and takes a year to do it. When I first saw that finding, I thought that this was really a trick question whose wording might have thrown respondents off track. So I went back to the original survey and looked at the question. It read: "The Earth orbits the sun and takes a year to do it. True or false?" That seems clear enough. And yet half of the American public got it wrong, and have gotten it wrong in virtually every survey that has been done.

In the 2001 survey, 53 percent of adults knew that human beings as we know them today developed from earlier species of animals. At the time, that seemed a great triumph; it was the first time that more than 50 percent of adults reported knowing that fact. But it was a short-lived blip in the American consciousness. In one 2004 survey, 45 percent of American adults agreed that God created humans in their present form less than 10,000 years ago.[6]

When the problem of a scientific disconnect with popular culture is exacerbated in the United States, it is also increasingly apparent elsewhere, including in Europe, where a recent study found that the number of people who felt the benefits of science outweighed the risks dropped 10 percent from 1992 to 2001, and where antievolution groups are making inroads in England, France, Denmark, and Holland.[7]

We face a basic problem in the public understanding of science. One contributing factor has been journalism. First of all, most journalists are simply not comfortable

enough with the basic principles of science to make pronouncements of the sort they might make on historical
or political issues. No mainstream paper or television
show would give any credibility to a group that denies
the Holocaust, for example. Yet I have only read once, in
the *New York Times,* a story in which the writer and
editor were willing to refer to evolution as the basis of
modern biology, rather than something that "many scientists accept."[8]

Beyond this relative neglect of science, journalists are
taught that there are always two sides to every story, so
when they do a science story—or any kind of story—they
try to air "both sides." Yet the very thing that makes
science unique and wonderful is that in most scientific
controversies, one side is simply wrong! Science works
precisely because it can prove some things absolutely
wrong. If certain contentions do not hold up with experiment, we can just stop talking about them.

If, however, one is looking for a contrary opinion, one
can always find a Ph.D. to provide one. Having a Ph.D. is
no guarantee against being a crackpot. But possession of
a doctoral degree can give the misimpression that such
contrary opinions may have equal weight in the community. So there is a fundamental tension between the way
scientists work and the way journalists work, and this
tension has complicated the reporting of science, particularly reporting about the conflict between evolution and
intelligent design.

What is intelligent design, anyway? Within the current
public debate it is framed in different ways. In fact, it is
not well defined precisely because it has not been subject,
as evolution has, for example, to years of detailed peer

review and examination. It can represent something as innocuous as the claim that the universe and life were designed with some purpose in mind, to the more explicit and seemingly scientific statement that existing cellular structures are too complex to be explained without design.[9] When examined closely, however, there is really one characteristic of all of the groups who are pushing intelligent design as a political issue. For them promoting intelligent design means simply being opposed to evolution.

But why devote such energy to opposing evolution? Now, that is a more fundamental question, and when we study it closely, we recognize that evolution is a straw man. What people are challenging is science itself and the methods by which it investigates the universe. And once again, the basis of that challenge is most often fear, in this case fear of the moral implications of science and its perceived challenge to religion.

In particular, because science does not explicitly incorporate God into its arguments, some groups believe that it is therefore inherently atheistic, and thus immoral.[10]

Years ago, my state of Ohio was one of the first to experience a concerted attack on science standards. A local group called Science Excellence for All Ohioans—an amazing name, given that the group was associated with televangelist James Dobson—accused in its pro-intelligent design literature: "Science standards use a little-known rule to censor the evidence of design. The rule, which is usually unstated, is often referred to as methodological naturalism."[11] We have a different name for it where I come from. It is called the scientific method.

Advocates of creationism and intelligent design ultimately stand opposed to the scientific method, because the scientific method is based on the assumption that natural effects have natural causes and that human beings can try to understand those causes. God is not mentioned; neither are spiritual issues. Obviously the idea that one might try to understand the workings of nature and make predictions about the world using empirically based knowledge is incompatible with some people's theological view of reality—and that is the heart of the problem. As long as science is viewed as a moral threat, and as long as the only solution to this threat is to replace naturalistic explanations of phenomena with theistic ones, the attack on science will continue.

The Discovery Institute, based in Seattle, is the driving force behind the media and political campaign against evolution.[12] It used to be called the Center for the Renewal of Science and Culture, but that was a very emotionally charged name, so they changed it.[13] When I first started to debate its representatives, I thought that they might be just a group of misinformed but well-meaning people. That is not the case. The people at the Discovery Institute know exactly what they are doing; they are well educated in media relations, very well funded, and will do and say whatever it takes to advance their agenda.

What is that agenda? Fortunately, they put it on the Internet some time ago, although it has since been removed. The "Wedge Strategy" was an internal planning document posted on the Center for the Renewal of Science and Culture's Web site in the late 1990s. Shortly after advocates for evolution discovered it in 1999, it was removed, though it is still available today on other sites.[14] The "Wedge Strategy" criticizes evolution as being scientifically suspect but moves quickly to a deeper preconception: "The proposition that human beings are created in the image of God is one of the bedrock principles on which Western civilization was built. This cardinal idea came under wholesale attack, drawing on the discoveries of modern science."[15] So science is the villain.

The document continues: "The Discovery Institute Center for the Renewal of Science and Culture seeks nothing less than the overthrow of materialism and its cultural legacies."[16] That is the core point, and in its way, it is much like the motivation that drove the Taliban—a view that materialism is intrinsically bad, that it has bad cultural legacies, and that everything bad in our society in some sense can be shown to result from science, which is seen as atheistic.

I do not believe that science must be inherently atheistic, in spite of the fact that there may be inherent and sometimes striking tensions between science and religion, as I shall describe. But ultimately the possible unilateral nonexistence of God or divine purpose simply is not a scientifically testable proposition.

It is not just right-wing lobbying groups or theologically naive individuals who insist on viewing science as a threat rather than a blessing. In 2005, after I wrote a piece in the *New York Times* about the fact that the Catholic Church accepts evolution as a fact within the context of their theological doctrine, a senior Catholic cardinal from Austria, a form student and confidant of Pope Benedict XVI, wrote an op-ed piece to counter my presumption.[17] His statement was particularly telling:

Defenders of neo-Darwinian dogma have often invoked the supposed acceptance—or at least acquiescence—of the Roman Catholic church when they defend their theory as somehow compatible with Christian faith.

But this is not true. The Catholic church, while leaving to science many details about the history of life on earth, proclaims that by the light of reason the human intellect can readily and clearly discern purpose and design in the natural world, including the world of living things.

Evolution in the sense of common ancestry might be true, but evolution in the neo-Darwinian sense—an unguided, unplanned process of random variation and natural selection—is not. Any system of thought that denies or seeks to explain away the overwhelming evidence for design in biology is ideology, not science.[18]

Aside from the fact that the cardinal's claim regarding reason and design is manifestly false, given that many scientists, based on a host of evidence from evolutionary biology, find that their reason discerns no evidence of design in the natural world, the cardinal more dangerously implies that the mere claim of nonevidence for design in biology is in fact tantamount to preaching atheism. I was sufficiently concerned about this misinterpretation of both science and theology that I, along with two prominent Catholic biologists, my colleague in the Terry lectureship Ken Miller, and Francisco Ayala, wrote a public letter to the pope to urge him to clarify the issue and not drive a new, unnecessary additional wedge between religion and science.[19] I am happy to report that since our letter, Cardinal Schönborn has in fact retracted much of his statement, and the official Vatican newspaper has reported that indeed evolution, as described by evolutionary biologists, without obvious divine intervention, is the best description of the observed diversity of life on earth.[20]

The negative impact of such religious assaults on science may be obvious as far as the effort to encourage scientific literacy among the public is concerned. However, I believe it does equal injury to theology. It is a disservice to all people of faith to argue that it is better to remain ignorant of the world than to risk the possibility that knowledge may undermine faith.

It is instructive to review briefly the history of creationist attacks on science education in the United States. In 1925 John T. Scopes was convicted of the crime of teaching evolution in a case that nevertheless heralded the beginning of the end of religiously enforced censorship of science teaching in the public schools.[21] Nevertheless, it may be surprising that it was not until 1968, the year before humans first landed on the moon, that the court, in the landmark Supreme Court decision *Epperson v. Arkansas,* ruled that states cannot ban the teaching of evolution on religious grounds. This decision has been upheld numerous times. In particular, though, in *Edwards v. Aguillard,* the Supreme Court affirmed that "creation science" is in fact religion and not science, but a dissenting opinion by Justice Antonin Scalia argued that nothing forbade schools from raising "evidence against evolution."[22] Of course, if there were such scientific evidence, scientists themselves would eagerly pounce upon it. But the lack of such evidence has not stopped numerous groups from jumping on this loophole as a way to suggest honest debate and controversy in an area in which no such controversy exists.

In 2002 the Ohio Board of Education was developing a new science curriculum, and there was a statewide controversy over whether to include intelligent design. Ken Miller and I debated two members of the Discovery Institute before the Board of Education and an audience of about 2,000 in Columbus, Ohio. Stephen Meyer, director of the Center for the Renewal of Science and Culture and a vice president of the Discovery Institute, made a bold rhetorical move that turned out to be the first appearance of a clever new theme in the marketing campaign for intelligent design: teaching the controversy.

Everyone expected Meyer to get up and say, "We want ID to be taught in schools." Instead he declared, "You know what? We're not dogmatic. We want to compromise. Let's just teach the controversy."[23] This was brilliant strategy. Meyer implied that there is a controversy, which there is not, and that there are grounds for compromise, which is also not true. Positioning the issue in this way automatically gave him the upper hand.

When the Board of Education finished the new science standards, we saw how effective Meyer's teach-the-controversy strategy had been.[24] Science advocates were congratulating themselves on a victory—for the first time in seventy years, the word *evolution* actually appeared in Ohio's science curriculum related to biology. But tacked on at the very end of the science standards was a phrase that required students to learn "how scientists continue to investigate and critically analyze aspects of evolutionary theory."[25]

Now there is nothing inherently wrong with that statement. The problem is that it was in the wrong place. A statement like that should appear at the beginning of the science curriculum and say something like, "Students should learn how scientists are continuing to investigate and critically analyze all scientific theories." After all, that is the way science works. Putting the statement so late in the document, where it pertained only to the science standards concerning evolution, had the effect of making evolution seem suspect. I and others so argued at the time, but the consensus seemed to be, "Nah, don't worry about it."

In short order, we learned that we should have worried about it. After the standards were approved, the Board of Education's curriculum committee produced a curriculum based on them. As we feared, instead of producing a lesson plan that showed how students were critically analyzing evolutionary theory, the committee produced a lesson plan critical of evolutionary theory. It was so badly flawed that the president of the National Academy of Sciences protested, as did many other individuals and groups.[26] I knew where we stood when I heard that one of the members of the board was asked why she had paid so little heed to the president of the NAS, and she replied, "I've never heard of the National Academy of Sciences. I thought it was some lobbying group." The proposed curriculum passed, and, though one of the committees that had drafted it denied that it was "a mandate to teach intelligent design,"[27] the Discovery Institute immediately proclaimed victory of the principle of teaching the controversy.[28]

Since the Dover decision, several groups examined the Ohio lesson plan and standards, and I wrote publicly that I felt that the standards were illegal for the same reason the judge in Dover determined that the Dover board statement did not respect the separation of church and state.[29]

I am very pleased to report that we were able to convince the governor to speak out and ultimately convince the Ohio Board of Education to remove both the offensive statement in the standards and the defective lesson plans. One may hope that this reflects a new, positive national trend, but I am leery of claiming victory. I have written elsewhere that the intelligent design movement in this country represents a marvelous example of evolution in action, as new incarnations arise and are tested out in the public relations battle against science.[30]

Policy makers deal with an enormous range of issues —not just political and economic, but philosophical, too. In the manufactured debate about evolution, questions will arise such as, "Is science without God incomplete?" "Is science without God immoral?" "Is there evidence for design?" Even if these questions are valid philosophical ones, they nevertheless do not motivate changing the nature of high-school science teaching.

The marketing campaign for intelligent design in this country has been well run and strategically ingenious. It is designed to exploit revered American values, including open-mindedness ("Look, we've got to just keep an open mind. We can't have this closed, dogmatic view of evolution."), honesty ("Let's be honest about the fact that most people don't believe in evolution."), and fairness ("Isn't it fair, if most people don't believe in evolution, that we teach alternatives in the schools?").

Particularly in its appeal to American intuitions about fairness, the public-relations campaign by advocates of intelligent design has won the day. When advocates of intelligent design put forward these ideas, most people say, "Why not?" In responding to this strategy, it is not enough for scientists to talk about the science. I think the argument that those who are interested in rationality have to present—and what we need to help policy makers realize—is that the intelligent design strategy is in fact closed-minded, dishonest, and unfair.

There are many ways we can point out that the intelligent design strategy is closed-minded. We can simply turn to the U.S. center of intelligent design activity, the Discovery Institute, and their Web documents to demonstrate that their version of intelligent design, unlike the version they hawk in public in which it is claimed that they are only interested in the best possible "science," is based on the presumption that science itself is immoral because it does not make reference to God; therefore, evolution is immoral, because it does not explicitly mention God either; therefore evolution must be wrong. That is closed-minded on its face. After all, the essence of open-mindedness is forcing your beliefs to conform to the evidence of observations, not forcing observations to conform to your beliefs. The intelligent design strategy pretty much demands the latter.

Demonstrating that the intelligent design strategy is dishonest requires a somewhat longer argument but is nonetheless straightforward. The dishonesty of intelligent design lies in the fact that its proponents point to a controversy when there really is no controversy. A friend of mine conducted an informal survey of more than ten million articles in major science journals during the past twelve years. Searching for the key word "evolution" pulled up 115,000 articles, most pertaining to biological evolution. Searching for "intelligent design" yielded eighty-eight articles. All but eleven of those were in engineering journals, where, of course, we hope that there is discussion of intelligent design! Of the eleven articles, eight were critical of the scientific basis for intelligent design theory, and the remaining three turned out to be articles in conference proceedings, not peer-reviewed research journals. So that is the extent of the "controversy" in the scientific literature. There is none.

When I raise this point in debate, advocates of intelligent design say, "Well, the reason it's not in the scientific literature is that scientists are closed-minded, and they won't let us get the stuff into the literature." I usually respond by challenging any opponent to prove that he or she has had more articles rejected by scientific journals than I have. So far, no one has risen to that challenge! The next defense of advocates of intelligent design is to say, "Okay, we do what Darwin did. We don't publish in journals. We produce books." Now, I shall grant that Darwin exerted much of his influence through his books, but he also made the Proceedings of the Royal Society![31]

Still, let us look into the honesty of the claim that an intelligent design "controversy" is alive and well in the world of books. One day in October 2005, I conducted my own informal survey of books that had not undergone peer review. Searching Amazon.com for the keyword "evolution" brought up 21,822 hits, of both books and articles. I scanned the list—I cannot claim to have done a serious, detailed study—and most titles appeared to pertain to the topic of biological evolution. When I searched for "intelligent design," there were 635 hits. About half of the titles were related to engineering. So about three hundred titles had to do with intelligent design related to the issue of evolution, and half of those were critical of intelligent design, leaving about 150 books and articles. Just for fun, I searched for the expression "alien abduction." There were 165 hits, which suggests that if public schools need to teach a "controversy," we might just as well teach about alien abduction.

Dishonesty is not the end of the matter. The intelligent design strategy is also unfair in a very particular way. Consider how real-world science gets done. Suppose you have a novel scientific claim. You do some research on it, either theoretical or experimental, which you then attempt to publish. You submit an article to journals, and the journals send it out to idiots called peer reviewers, and those idiots tell you why you are wrong, and then you have to fight with them and tell them why they are idiots, and it goes on and on. If you are lucky, you get published.

But being published is not itself much. Lots of nonsense gets published (as some may be tempted to point out upon reading this piece). But, if your work is interesting, other people will begin to look at it and do follow-up research. If it is really interesting, you will build a scientific consensus, which may take ten, twenty, thirty, or forty years. Only then does your work get mentioned in high-school textbooks. In my own field of physics, the material in today's textbooks is easily twenty to thirty years out of date—because that is how science works.

Intelligent design advocates want to skip all the intermediate steps. They want to take their theory straight into high-school textbooks. And that is not fair. Advocates of intelligent design are unwilling to play by the same rules as scientists. If they believe intelligent design is a scientific theory, they should welcome the requirement that they go through all the steps that other scientists have to go through before their work makes its way into textbooks.

I have tried to show, then, that the intelligent design strategy is closed-minded, dishonest, and unfair. But there is another issue we need to explain to policy makers —and to journalists, as I mentioned above—and that is that conventional American intuitions about fairness are simply out of place in genuine scientific debate. Science itself is not fair—and that very fact may be science's greatest legacy. In science, not all ideas are treated equally. The geocentric view is not treated equally today, because we know that the sun does not go around the earth. Science's power lies precisely in its ability to prove false things to be false.

At this point, policy makers might ask, "But what about the fact that at least half of the American public doesn't believe in evolution?" Public opinion about evolution is actually far more discouraging than that. In a June 2005 Harris Poll, 54 percent of respondents said that they disbelieved in evolution.[32] Only 38 percent accepted it. Asked what they do believe about human origins, only 22 percent of respondents said human beings evolved from earlier species. In contrast, 64 percent said human beings were created directly by God, and 10 percent said they believed in intelligent design. According to this survey, three-quarters of Americans reject the theory of evolution. Asked what should be taught in pubic schools, a mere 12 percent of respondents said that only evolution should be taught. Twice as many, 23 percent, thought only creationism should be taught. Most of the rest, 55 percent in fact, thought creationism, evolution, and intelligent design should be taught—on grounds of fairness, of course. So how can we respond when a policy maker cites this sort of data and says, "Look, why not teach all three?"

Let us look back at one of the statistics cited earlier. Only 50 percent of American adults know that the earth orbits the sun and takes a year to do it. Therefore, if we are doing things democratically and fairly, should we not therefore teach geocentric cosmology in physics classes? The point that seems to be lost on many people—and the point that advocates of intelligent design hope will stay lost—is that the purpose of education is not to validate ignorance; it is to overcome it. If we are doing a crummy job of teaching science in America—and we are—then we need to do a better job in teaching many different kinds of science, including evolutionary biology. Far from watering it down or teaching a nonexistent controversy, we need to teach science better.

Even conceding all the arguments above, some may still contend that even if intelligent design is a straw man, there can still be benefit in teaching it. If teachers present the theory of intelligent design and show why it is scientific garbage, students can learn something about critical thinking. This is not, in principle, an irrational argument. But why teach critical thinking by attacking a straw man in the science classroom when real scientific controversies are plentiful? In physics, there are huge debates about the nature of gravity (indeed, there are far more papers in print questioning Newton's law of gravity or Einstein's general theory of relativity than there are questioning evolution) and the validity of quantum mechanics. In biology, there are important debates about the nature of random mutation and natural selection and the importance of one versus the other in driving evolution. These are real controversies, any one of them with a literature far larger than the "literature" on intelligent design. The problem, of course, is that to appreciate fully which issues are controversial and which are not, one must first learn the basic science.

There is another claim made in the attack on evolution that resonates with many people, but which completely misrepresents what science is all about. As John Bacon, a Kansas State School Board member with an unfortunate name given his apparent vast ignorance of science, has been quoted in the *New York Times* as saying: "I can't understand what they are squealing about. [Millions or billions of years ago] I wasn't here and neither were they!"[33]

The claim that evolution is "historical science" because much of the evidence for evolution over the earth's history is based on past fossils et cetera, and therefore that evolution is somehow "suspect," completely misses the point. Science is not just a story about the past, so that different people can tell different stories, evolution, young-earth creationism, et cetera, and we can all live in harmony. Science is a story with *consequences,* called predictions. Historical science makes predictions about the future, not the past. It makes predictions about observations that have not yet been performed! That is how theories live and die. And that is why, when I recently visited a newly built "Creation Museum," I tried to tell people that to accept the ludicrous idea that the earth is 6,000 years old requires them to deny the basic features of chemistry, biology, physics, astronomy, geology, et cetera. Moreover, these very features are responsible for most of modern technology. If they were incorrect, planes, trains, automobiles, televisions, et cetera, simply would not work as advertised, or rather would have to depend upon new miracles every single day.

One can put this another way. *All* science is historical science. Everything in chemistry and physics, for example, is based on *past* observations. What makes these sciences is that one then makes predictions about the results of future experiments that allows one to develop powerful new tools that affect the human condition. Even sciences that do not seem as historical as evolutionary biology often are. For example, every time we look at the sun, we are seeing light that was emitted from its surface about eight minutes ago. Well, that is not the distant past, but in fact, we know, from our studies of the solar interior, that the light energy actually takes about one million years to get out of the sun after it is released in nuclear reactions deep in the solar core. Thus, we are literally looking back a million years when we see the sun and study it.

Perhaps the last, most desperate resort of the advocate of intelligent design is to demand to know why we care so much about textbook stickers, a few sentences read before class, or whatever the next intelligent design initiative may turn out to be. For some, it is an issue of church-state separation, but that is not my bottom line. To me, the crucial point is that whenever teachers are made to soft-pedal evolution or teach a controversy that is not there, we are forcing teachers to lie. The minute we force teachers to lie in one place, we make it easier to force them to lie in others. That kind of blurring of truth may be the greatest threat to our democracy. I do not view religion as the greatest threat to our democracy. It is rather lying and ignorance that are the greatest threats to our democracy.

At this point, it is appropriate to turn to a more subtle issue, and one about which I think many scientists tend to distort the nature of science as much as some on the other side of the science versus religion debate do.

We first need to be clear about the fact that there are some innate tensions between science and religion, described best, I believe, by the physicist Steven Weinberg in the quotation that opened this essay. While he is no friend of religion, I remind you that he nevertheless said, "Science does not make it impossible to believe in God." But he also added a phrase that is equally important: "It just makes it possible to not believe in God."[34] And that is really profoundly significant because until you have science, everything is a miracle. But when you have science, it is possible to accept a world in which everything is governed by the laws of nature.

The fact, however, that science makes it possible to not believe in God is often incorrectly interpreted, at least in my opinion, by those on both sides of the science-religion debate to imply that science requires an atheistic conclusion.

In this regard, I want to turn to one of the sources of great tension, evident in the statement of Cardinal Schönborn cited earlier. This is the question of the "evidence" for design in nature. The cardinal seemed to imply that if science does not validate an explicit design in nature then it must be wrong, while many scientists who find no such explicit design argue that therefore there must be no divine purpose. I believe both points of view are logically inconsistent.

First, inferring the existence of design is notably difficult, and notably subjective. I can display what may appear to be pictures of beautiful Christmas ornaments and people will say that they are clearly designed. In fact the pictures would really be electron micrographs of snowflakes. There is not intelligent design there; there is chemistry and physics describing how molecules with bond patterns of water can form crystal structures that produce beautiful patterns when liquid freezes. Presented with human structures, like the geodesic domes of Buckminster Fuller, one can clearly infer evidence for design. But you can see the same patterns in a molecule called Buckminsterfullerene (Carbon-60), which was discovered accidentally in soot, and which may someday have important technological applications.[35] Few people would argue that soot is so designed.

By the same token, while much of the beauty of the animal kingdom may look on the surface like pure genius of design, there are manifest examples that should lead one to question this notion, beyond the simple fact that evolution provides a perfectly natural mechanism for living organisms to have the appearance of design. For example, almost all species that have ever lived on earth are now extinct. Is that good evidence for design? There are many more examples, from the anatomy of the human eye, to dual use of our throats for breathing and eating, that present manifest evidence of what one might call "poor design," but which can be understood in terms of historical evolutionary remnants.

This notion of design in nature is therefore very subtle. But even if we determine, as some think science has clearly done, that there is not manifest evidence for design in nature, the fact that they may see no explicit evidence for design in nature does not imply with certainty that there was no design. I believe that many scientists who are responding to the current religious attacks on science seem to miss this point, which I believe was put best by Carl Sagan in a different context (discussing the possible existence of alien intelligence in the cosmos), when he said, "absence of evidence need not be evidence of absence."[36]

While science can therefore never unambiguously resolve the question of purpose in the universe in the negative, it should be added that science could uncover positive evidence of divine guidance and purpose, if it were attainable. For example, if tomorrow night we look up at the stars and they have been rearranged into a pattern that reads, "I am here," I think that even the most hardnosed scientific skeptic would suspect something was up.

The fact that such evidence has not turned up among the millions and millions of pieces of data that we have gleaned about the natural world over centuries of exploration leads many scientists to the not unnatural conclusion that it is unlikely that there is any divine purpose in the universe. But of course there can be a whole universe of difference between "unlikely" and "impossible."

Ultimately, what is most important to understand is that the science can be independent of questions of purpose and design. The best example I know of is a story relating to Georges Lemaître, the Belgian priest and physicist who was the first one to demonstrate that Einstein's general relativity theoretically implied that there was a Big Bang beginning to the universe.[37] When Lemaître first made this argument, Einstein, who, like most other scientists at the time felt that the universe was static and eternal, scoffed at the idea.[38] But eventually it was shown to be correct.

After successfully confronting the conventional scientific wisdom that the universe was eternal, and instead demonstrating that it was likely to have had a beginning in the finite past—indeed, one that could certainly be said to be born in light—Lemaître was hailed by many, including Pope Pius XII himself, as having scientifically proved Genesis.[39]

Lemaître, however, was convinced that it was inappropriate to use the Big Bang as a basis for theological pronouncements. He initially inserted, then ultimately removed, a paragraph in the draft of the 1931 paper on the Big Bang remarking on the possible theological consequences of his discovery. In the end, he said, "As far as I can see, such a theory remains entirely outside of any metaphysical or religious question."

Lemaître thus grasped the key point that is often missed in the current public debate about evolution. The Big Bang is not a metaphysical theory but a scientific one: namely, one that derives from equations that have been measured to describe the universe, and that makes predictions that one can test. It is certainly true that one can reflect on the existence of the Big Bang to validate the notion of creation, and with that the notion of God. But one can equally well interpret the equations as dispensing with any need for God. The point is that both such metaphysical speculations lie outside of the theory itself, which makes predictions and either agrees with the data or does not.

This argument is not meant to imply that metaphysical speculation is not important, just that it is not science. In this regard scientists have responsibility not to overstep their bounds. The success of science does not mean that it encompasses the entire human intellectual experience. We have to worry about what some people call "science versus scientism," which I take to mean arguing that if something is not scientifically demonstrable, it is not worth considering. The question of purpose in the universe is generally a philosophical question, not a scientific one.

There is, moreover, a strategic issue here, which I have discussed at length with my scientific colleague Richard Dawkins.[40] As I have argued, if we do not see design in nature, and I certainly do not, that does not mean that it is not there somewhere. But in general, arguing *against* something is never particularly productive, especially when dealing with the public and their hesitant attitudes toward science, especially when they perceive it to be infringing upon religion's turf. The strategy of focusing on telling people what not to believe is less compelling that telling them how fascinating the world is based on the knowledge that science has uncovered. Thus, not only is it not particularly scientific to harp on the perceived nonexistence of God based on the results of science, it achieves less of significance in terms of education. To be fair, I should add that Dawkins has countered that it is important to raise consciousness about the viability and the acceptability of the alternative of not believing in God.[41]

Regardless of one's strategy in demonstrating that science should be not a threat but a wonderful gift, we need to get across the notion that the universe uncovered by science is a profoundly remarkable place. Science education should awaken American students to that fact. The cosmic story of the history of the universe, which I tried to outline in a personal way in my book *Atom,* is every bit as awe-inspiring as any religious account of creation, and probably more mind-expanding.[42]

In this regard, let me turn to my last point. Science may be viewed by some as a threat to faith, but as long as religious faith remains a core part of organized human society—and I do not foresee that as changing in the near future—science can play a key role by actually enriching this faith.

This possibility has been recognized by theologians from Saint Augustine to Moses Maimonides, and by Pope John Paul II and the Dalai Lama, as well as by scientists from Galileo onward. Science describes how the world works, and anyone who believes that it reflects a divine plan should recognize that by learning about nature one can come closer to understanding its ultimate meaning, if any. Einstein argued, in the quote at the beginning of this essay, that blind respect for authority is the greatest enemy of truth.[43] I believe that science can inform faith precisely by opposing blind, unquestioning, and often incorrect belief.

The earth is not 6,000 years old, the sun did not stand still in the sky, homosexuality is not an abomination (i.e., it is not *unnatural* in that it occurs with reasonable frequencies in a number of different species), women are not subservient chattel, as evidenced in the actions described in the Old Testament. Recognizing that the Bible, the Koran, and other ancient religious documents are historical documents reflecting the understanding of nature and divinity by individuals who lived in societies where modern scientific knowledge was not available is a vital part of understanding and interpreting these documents. And to be more democratic in giving offense, and not just focus on past Judeo-Christian myths, the Kennewick man, a 9,000-year-old skeleton discovered in Washington State, is not an Umatilla Indian and we should not have wasted any time when the Umatilla tribe wanted to keep that wonderful skeleton away from scientific exploration.[44]

It is not a threat to faith to correct factual errors based on modern knowledge. Maimonides understood this when he wrote, "The Scriptures are absolutely true. However, if the Scriptures appear to disagree with the results of scientific investigation, one should re-examine one's interpretation of the Scriptures."[45]

The universe is a remarkable place without all the nonsense we impose upon it. That is really what our goal should be to explain to people. You do not need the junk to make the universe interesting, satisfying, and uplifting. And science can help us distinguish what is junk.

Operationally this principle is manifested by the fact that science works. Our technological society is based on science, and our future depends on teaching our children the best science we can in order to prepare them to face the real changes of the dangerous world of the twenty-first century. By "dangerous," I refer not to terrorism but to the impending consequences of what humanity has spent the past couple of centuries doing to nature. The only way our children will be able to address real issues like those is to understand them.

When, moreover, there is a clear and present natural threat, people instinctively turn to science. George Bush talked about how we should teach both sides of the debate about intelligent design. Yet when the avian flu arose, he spoke about how we have to worry about how quickly it is mutating between birds and humans. You never heard him, or anyone else, say, "It's been designed to kill us, let's forget it."

But in recognizing the power of modern science, we should nevertheless retain an appropriate sense of humility. Science is a way of knowing that has raised human civilization up tremendously, but science alone cannot reveal everything that many humans feel is worth knowing about the universe. Albert Einstein stated this sentiment in a way that resonates strongly with my own growing sense of understanding of the role of science and religion in human experience: "What separates me from most so-called atheists is a feeling of utter humility toward the unattainable secrets of the harmony of the universe."[46]

Whatever unattainable secrets remain, I believe that only if we remain willing to accept the universe for what it is, without fear or prejudice, can we build a truly just society. Science is not a threat to a moral world. Quite the contrary; science has an ethos based on honesty, open-mindedness, creativity, egalitarianism, and full disclosure. If those things were realized as thoroughly in the rest of the world as they already are in science, the world would be a better place.

Science is not the enemy. But faith also is not the enemy. The enemy is ignorance. Ignorance breeds fear, and fear is the source of much conflict, including the skirmishes between science and religion that I have described in this essay.

And for those who find as a scary prospect a mysterious universe where we are not given all of the answers by God, we should remind them that mystery can nevertheless be a wonderful thing. It is perhaps appropriate to turn once again to Albert Einstein, with whom I began this essay, who said, "The fairest thing we can experience is the mysterious. It is the fundamental emotion that stands at the cradle of true art, and true science."[47]

No Contradictions Here
Science, Religion, and the
Culture of All Reasonable Possibilities

ROBERT WUTHNOW

In seeking perspective on recent controversies about religion and science, one can hardly do better than the wisdom provided by that bible of guidance and revelation for academics, the *New York Times*. In its coverage of litigation about the teaching of intelligent design, of school board decisions about evolution, and of policy debates about stem cell research and genetic engineering, the nation's favorite arbiter of elite opinion has documented beyond doubt that questions about the respective roles of science and religion remain of great public interest. It is this public interest—or, more precisely, the cultural role—of these controversies on which I wish to focus. What fascinates me about the *New York Times'* coverage is not its reportage or even its editorials, but the letters it chooses to print from its readers.

Unsurprisingly, many of the letters speak in favor of science, while others side clearly with religion. The former variously associate science with hard evidence, discovery, and progressive thinking in contrast with the ludicrous, disheartening, and even dangerous claims of religious ideologues. The latter question whether scientific facts are as firmly established as scientists claim and worry about the moral implications of science. A few accuse scientists of promoting an agenda of unfettered atheism. But far more interesting are the letters that seek to reconcile science and religion. For example, a reader from Minneapolis writes: "In my view, there is no contradiction between evolution and religion. One explains how, and the other explains why."[1] A scientist in Los Angeles observes, "Science is a tool for furthering human understanding of the natural world, and as such can co-exist with religion."[2] A reader in New Jersey elaborates: "Science is about the natural, material world; religion is about the supernatural and spiritual. Science operates mainly with numbers; religion with words." He concludes: "In short, they are separate but equal."[3]

These readers are the voices of reason, the defenders of a middle ground threatened as much by the simplistic proponents of science as by the radical claims of religious extremists. Theirs is a both-and rather than an either-or world. They are in distinguished company. They stand with Albert Einstein, who famously remarked, "Science without religion is lame, religion without science is blind," and with Stephen Jay Gould, who has argued that science tells us what the universe is made of while religion deals with ultimate meaning and moral value.[4] They rise above the fray, so to speak, refusing to opt for the pre-defined positions presented to them, instead preferring to question the very terms in which the debate has been cast. They are what we train our students at Yale and Princeton to be. They are capable of seeing both sides of an argu-ment, of parsing what at first appear to be irreconcilable views and thus transforming black and white into shades of gray. Their approach is so attractive, so thoroughly educated, and so reassuringly American.

It has not been popular, at least in my discipline of sociology, for scholars to be interested in studying people who espouse a language of moderation and reason. That language is too much our own to feel comfortable exam-ining it critically. The popular tactic is to start from the supposition that proponents on the religious side of these—and most other—arguments are so downright strange as to deserve most of our attention. Thus, we dig a bit and find that they are really expressing some eco-nomic or political grievance that they are too dumb to recognize themselves, or worse, are being led astray by clever political operatives or self-aggrandizing religious leaders. For instance, in *What's the Matter with Kansas?* Thomas Frank, a native of that state who fled to the big time in Chicago, argues that Kansans vote Republican because they are obsessed with keeping evolution out of their schools and putting prayer back in, whereas voting Democrat would be better for their state's economy.[5] Jayhawkers are bargaining away the chance to give their children a better future, he says, by focusing more at-tention on moral battles than on good jobs and better schools.

Thomas Frank is perhaps not the best example of serious scholarship, since his book is candidly autobiographical and impressionistic. Yet it is worth noting that
his work has been warmly embraced in the social science
community.[6] A more thoroughly academic example can
be found in the work of sociologist Amy Binder, whose
book *Contentious Curricula* examines creationist controversies.[7] Binder argues that creationists are cleverer than
the naive reader may have supposed. Leaders "frame" appeals in religious terms when speaking to church groups
but downplay this rhetoric when talking to the media or
in the courts. They strategically mobilize against school
boards rather than against larger governing bodies because it takes fewer resources to do so. It helps when
they win elections to these boards. It hurts when school
administrators muscle creationists aside with assertions
about separation of church and state.

It is understandable that scholars focus on what they
perceive as deviant behavior. The very idea of a few citizens in out-of-the-way places like Kansas and Dover,
Pennsylvania, promoting strange ideas sends journalists
and social scientists scurrying to study this quaint phenomenon.[8] It is as if the Amish suddenly ran a candidate
for president. What would the world be like if these
creationists—whom their own neighbors describe as the
laughingstock of the world—succeeded in eliminating
science from the curriculum? Perhaps there is something
to be learned here about the peculiarities of American
culture, just as there is from studying serial killers.

If the goal is to understand American culture, it would
nevertheless seem strange to focus on the periphery and
neglect the center. The both-and position expressed in

thoughtful letters to the editor is held by a large share of the American public. In public opinion polls, this middle ground is favored by a majority or large minority of the public, depending on the wording of specific questions. For instance, a CBS News survey conducted in 2005 found that 67 percent of the public believes it is "possible to believe in both God and evolution," while only 29 percent thought this was not possible.[9]

The sheer reasonableness of the both-and approach, though, necessarily raises two interesting puzzles. First, why is it that science and religion appear to be in conflict at all? Is it that the antagonists who perpetrate these struggles are less reasonable than everyone else? Is it perhaps true that they are simply duped by their leaders? If it is so sensible to argue that science and religion are simply different, would it not be more likely that conflict between the two would be nonexistent? Pursuing these questions will provide a way of examining afresh why religion and science might not be so easily reconciled, even for reasonable people. Once we have considered these possibilities, though, a different puzzle arises: Why are the conflicts between science and religion as infrequent as they are? This question will take us into the larger terrain of contemporary culture where we can view the assumptions that undergird our conviction that reasonable people can simply resolve their differences if they bring enough gray matter to the table.

Religion and Science as Separate Spheres

A useful place to begin is the idea commonly known in sociological theory as institutional differentiation. The idea of institutional differentiation, simply put, is that the various spheres of social life are more distinct and specialized than they probably were in earlier times when societies were smaller and less complex. For instance, Max Weber argued that one of the important preconditions for the rise of modern capitalism was the separation of paid labor from households. This separation of spheres, Weber suggested, made it possible for labor to be governed with greater attention to rewarding productivity than was the case when workers were also family members.[10] The emergence of modern science in seventeenth-century Europe is typically regarded as another example of institutional differentiation. Although its rise may have been facilitated by religion, science became an autonomous sphere, capable of setting its own agenda and determining for itself what activities were worth pursuing.[11]

If science and religion are distinct institutions, then this is further reason to believe that potential conflict can be overcome by recognizing their differences. These are not merely conceptual differences, such as one of emphasizing the natural or supernatural, but also of social arrangements themselves. Scientific academies do science and religious organizations do religion. Scientists do not preach and preachers are ill-suited to conduct scientific research. Of course it might be objected that greater specialization requires greater interaction across spheres—a point Emile Durkheim emphasized in describing the "organic solidarity" that arises from people with different occupations becoming interdependent.[12]

This argument needs to be pushed further, though. A baker and butcher might be mutually dependent, but it is less clear that science and religion bear the same relationship to one another. A better analogy would be two all-purpose delis, one specializing in bread and the other in meat, but both seeking to expand. Science and religion come into conflict because neither stays neatly in its respective sphere. As Gili S. Drori and his co-authors observe in their recent empirical study of the global expansion of science as a cultural form, "A reasonable way to interpret the long history of conflict between scientific and religious models is to see these institutions as competing on the same ground, rather than operating in different domains."[13]

Overlapping and Ambiguous Domains

As science has grown, its autonomy has been compromised by the very fact that it influences more aspects of social life and in turn is dependent on a wider array of social, economic, and political resources. The patronage that supported Kepler's observatory in Denmark, Galileo's research in Italy, the Royal Society in London, and the French Academy of Sciences in Paris came from royal coffers, the Medici, and other wealthy individuals such as the Dukes of Savoy and Tuscany.[14] Only much later did governments require average citizens to support science through taxes and expose their children to science in public schools. The advance of science was an act not only of intellectual achievement but also of political displacement. "The three estates of the realm," wrote Don K. Price in his memorable account of this transition, "were the clergy, the nobility, and the burgesses." The privileges of all three were abolished. "But now," Price observed, "the results of scientific advance have been to require federal support of education and the appropriation of a tithe of the federal budget for research and development."[15]

The idea that science merely describes the natural world, leaving questions about purpose and worth to religion, is simply untrue. The sharp rise in developing nations' initiation of government-sponsored science ministries and participation in international scientific organizations illustrates the extent to which being "modern" and "progressive" requires at least a symbolic commitment to science. Being an educated person does not require knowing anything about religion but does involve taking courses in science, passing examinations testing one's familiarity with scientific thinking, and being respectful toward science in one's work and at parties. In these ways, science shapes the cultural norms that serve as standards of self-worth. Personal identity is deeply influenced in other ways by scientific discoveries. The meaning of human personhood is profoundly shaped by how humanity itself is located in an evolutionary chain or an expanding view of nearly infinite galaxies.

For its part, religion may appear in many instances to be in retreat, but it too expands periodically out of its earlier domain. The role of Darwinism in the rise of late nineteenth-century Protestant fundamentalism is a commonly cited example. Fundamentalism was as surely an attempt to be scientific as it was an effort to resist science. Millenarian predictions about the fulfillment of biblical prophecies gained popularity as these arguments relied more heavily on numeric calculations and new certainties about the orderly progression of time.[16] During the 1950s, religious organizations drew significantly from the social sciences (especially psychology) and from the expanding mental health movement in developing new and more highly specialized programs of pastoral counseling.[17] The more recent emergence of creation *science* and of arguments about intelligent design, borrowing as they do from scientific studies and from critical discussions within the scientific literature, could be considered another such example.

The interaction that results when science and religion expand into each other's turf is more complex even than this image of competition implies because the boundaries defining the two spheres are themselves matters of negotiation. What Thomas F. Gieryn calls "boundary work" consists of scientists' ongoing efforts to create a favorable "public image for science by contrasting it favorably to non-scientific intellectual or technical activities."[18] In Victorian England, for instance, scientists publicly ridiculed church leaders who prayed for God's intervention against the cholera epidemic of 1866, denounced prayer as a form of superstition, and charged the church with standing in the way of scientific progress. Gieryn suggests that religion bashing actually served scientists well, meaning that in a convoluted way religion as an enemy of science is also its friend. Rather than depicting religion as something different from science but useful in its own way, scientists characterized it as pseudo-science based on false empirical claims. That such uses of religion by scientists continue is readily apparent. Writing in the *New York Times,* evolutionary biologist Olivia Judson argued, for instance, that an understanding of evolution was vital to guarding against a flu pandemic and "saving the lives of tens of millions of people." By implication,

religionists themselves might be responsible if a flu pandemic did occur. "Let's not strip evolution from the textbooks," she wrote, "or banish it from the class, or replace
it with ideologies born of wishful thinking. If we do, we
might find ourselves facing the consequences of natural
selection."[19]

Boundary work suggests conscious and even malicious manipulation of the turf wars between religion and
science. It is also the case, though, that boundary questions become important because definitions of "religion"
and "science" are themselves subject to cultural construction. For instance, popular assertions about religion typically assume that it is readily defined by belief in God or
resort in some other way to arguments about the supernatural. Yet scholars of religion seldom define it in those
terms. Clifford Geertz's well-worn definition, for example, refers neither to God nor to the supernatural but
emphasizes symbols, powerful and long-lasting motivations, and conceptions of a general order of existence
clothed in an aura of factuality.[20] Would that definition
not apply equally to some understandings of science?

Lest it be assumed that religion is somehow unique in
being subject to such definitional ambiguities, it is worth
noting that science too has come under scrutiny for the
same reasons. What counts as scientific fact is by no
means dictated only by nature itself. "Scientific activity is
not 'about nature,'" Bruno Latour and Steve Woolgar
write in their influential ethnographic study of laboratory life, "it is a fierce fight to *construct* reality."[21] They do
not mean that scientists falsify their observations or fab-
ricate reality from thin air. They do show through numerous examples how scientific conclusions are influ-

NO CONTRADICTIONS HERE   165

enced by the availability or unavailability of instruments, how powerful teams impose standards that may reduce the ability of other teams to compete, and how tentative statements preclude the possibility of pursuing other reasonable lines of investigation.

The upshot of these examples is that neither science nor religion can be quite as easily compartmentalized into separate and noncompeting domains as our both-and commentators want to believe. It is the case that ambiguous conceptual categories can be the starting place for more nuanced arguments about similarities and differences. The more relevant point, however, is that ambiguity also opens the door for continuing conflict. It is simply impossible to look back at some historic event and conclude that the debate between religion and science was finally resolved. As long as the two have fuzzy edges, proponents, antagonists, and bystanders in the general public will be able to contest where one domain should end and the other begin. The likelihood of such contestation increases, as I have suggested, because religion and science are never static. Indeed, both struggle to assert themselves as legitimate ways of addressing important issues and thus as legitimate claimants of social resources.

Hermeneutics of Suspicion

Paul Ricoeur's hermeneutics of suspicion is usually associated with the critique of religion that one finds in Marx, Nietzsche, and Freud. These masters of suspicion, as Ricoeur termed them, unveiled the illusory character of religion by showing that it concealed political and economic interests.[22] To see reality clearly, one needed to unmask the false perceptions of religion. Yet in our time it might be argued that this skeptical attitude toward religion has also extended to science. Power and privilege most certainly lie with the scientific estate as much today as they did with religion in the past. The high esteem in which the public holds science and scientists, if polls are believed, is tempered with the populist ambivalence that colors public attitudes toward all elites. Admiration bleeds easily into envy and further into disdain. If a segment of the religious community stands ready to battle science over evolution and genetic engineering, this broader hermeneutics of suspicion is almost certainly a predisposing factor.

Science is sometimes popularly regarded as the great savior, bringing hope for conquering illnesses and inventing labor-saving technology, but its image has also been tarnished. Critical discussions of science seldom pass up the opportunity to connect it with the development of the atomic bomb. In medical research, the infamous Tuskegee experiment in which some four hundred poor black men were never told they had syphilis and never treated for it, all in the name of research, is often mentioned. Environmental concerns have also affected public perceptions of science. "Ever since the publication of Rachel Carson's *Silent Spring* in the 1960s," former National Science Foundation director Richard C. Atkinson recalls, "there was a growing feeling abroad that the purity of science . . . was not quite as pure as it had seemed."[23]

An additional factor that aggravates the potential conflict between religion and science is that relatively few scientists are religious (at least in conventional ways). For instance, in a recent national survey of physicists, chemists, and biologists at elite research universities, only 8 percent said they had no doubts about God's existence, while 38 percent said they did not believe in God, and another 29 percent said they did not know if there is a God and believed there was no way to find out. In the same survey, 55 percent said they had no religious affiliation and only 16 percent attended religious services at least once a month.[24] These figures underscore the sharp differences that exist between scientists and the general public, where, for instance, only 7 percent can be regarded as atheists or agnostics.[25] If the public imagines that scientists' personal views influence their scholarship, then perceptions of conflict between religion and science would not be surprising.

A further confounding aspect of the relationship between religion and science is what is sometimes referred to as the hubris of science. Having considered Einstein's remark about the complementarities of religion and science, we need also to recall Abraham Heschel's rejoinder: "Hubris, the tragic sin of our time, is the conviction that there exist only laws of nature and technology."[26] Heschel's view is currently echoed in Internet blogs, where this perception of science surfaces freely. "I'm skeptical of scientists and technologists designing animals or genes or drugs or anything else that nature already does perfectly," one blogger remarks. In this anonymous blogger's view, scientists are drunk on hubris, in it for the money or their own glory, and sadly incapable of any humility. A less emotionally tinged argument emerges in the writing of Annie Dillard, the Pulitzer Prize–winning author of *Pilgrim at Tinker Creek*, which was widely praised for its extraordinary sensitivity to the complexity of the natural world. In *For the Time Being*, Dillard adds a more explicitly theological, cultural, and historical dimension to her reflections. Noting that our time has produced antibiotics, silicon chips, men on the moon, and spliced genes, she asks, "Are not our heightened times the important ones?" She might have added that after eons of evolution, suddenly we, through the explorations of science, are now the first ever to have grasped that process. Surely science has taught us so much in the past century that we could not possibly be wrong about what we know. Do we not have good reason to think that our time is especially significant? Her answer: "These times of ours are ordinary times, a slice of life like any other. Who can bear to hear this, or who will consider it?"[27]

Perceptions of scientific hubris remind us that cultural disputes with science are by no means limited to those involving religion. The "two cultures" that C. P. Snow described in the 1950s were not science and religion but science and the humanities or, more specifically, literary intellectuals. Snow is generally interpreted as having argued for greater interaction between science and the humanities (a supporter of the both-and view), but his remarks about science also convey understated criticism. "The scientific culture," he wrote, "is expansive, not restrictive, confident at the roots, the more confident after its bout of Oppenheimerian self-criticism, certain that history is on its side, impatient, intolerant."[28] Snow's concerns continue to be voiced in larger criticisms about the moral fragmentation of a culture in which the can-do attitude of science presumably overwhelms questions about deeper values. Noting contemporary society's assumption "that *every* problem facing mankind is susceptible to technological intervention and control," Roger Kimball writes, for instance, that "the temptation to reduce culture to a reservoir of titillating pastimes is all but irresistible." In this critique, science is not so much the only source of cultural deterioration but a contributor to the malaise that includes drugs, violence, promiscuity, and an insatiable desire for gratification.[29]

Why the Conflict Is Not Worse

Having considered the reasons to expect conflict between science and religion, I turn now to the second question: With such potential for conflict, why is it that the actual skirmishes between science and religion have been relatively rare? Why is it that among the more than 14,000 school districts in the United States, only a few have become involved in litigation about evolution and intelligent design? With such a large number of religious organizations and so many people believing in God and creationism, would it not have been reasonable to expect a great deal more conflict with science than there has been? What accounts for the fact that most Americans seem content to believe that there are no contradictions between science and religion? This capacity to look at the world in both-and terms is, in my view, the telling feature of American culture, not the occasional fisticuffs between religionists and scientists.

Let us acknowledge that the ease with which we reconcile seemingly opposing points of view may well be rooted in something more pervasive than American culture itself. Public opinion researchers have long recognized that people give inconsistent responses in surveys without feeling a need to reconcile the apparent contradictions.[30] Anthropologists have argued that one of the central features of tribal rituals is their capacity to hold in tension two seemingly opposite beliefs or practices.[31] Cognitive dissonance theory, though no longer as uncritically accepted among psychologists as it once was, asserts that people adjust their beliefs when asked to perform tasks that deviate from their values.[32] The common thread in all this research is that the mind is malleable and finds ways to create order—or escape having to create order—when tension arises.

Yet the point is not *that* people reconcile themselves to seemingly contradictory beliefs or statements about the world, but *how* they do this. The capacity to create consistency may be cognitively available, but the manner in which this order-imposing process is carried out is cultural. In the case of both-and views about science and religion, resolution does not come by adjusting one's views to be more compatible with science or with religion. Nor does it involve simply keeping the two apart. The cultural work involved is more complex and, although it includes specific ideas about religion and science, it is also associated with broader ways in which our culture enables us to minimize conflict.

Culture is above all language, and language provides the first means of dealing with apparent contradictions. An example that I have examined in some detail in another context is the discursive negotiation of tension in American culture between individualism and altruism. The two are not mirror opposites, any more than science and religion are, but they do run in opposing directions. Individualism connotes looking out for one's self-interest, whereas altruism means putting another's needs ahead of one's own. American culture emphasizes both. In personal interviews, altruists who are also individualistic manage the potential conflict by employing a number of discursive devices, one of the most common of which is multivocality—literally, speaking through the voice of different characters within the space of a few sentences. For instance, a person might say: "I help at the soup kitchen one night a week and people there tell me, 'You are really a kind-hearted person,' but I say, 'No, not really. I get a lot out of being here.' I have to admit, though, sometimes I'd rather stay home and relax." Although the remarks are all uttered by one person, the different voices involved permit the complexity of the issue to be displayed. The speaker at once affirms that she does engage in helping behavior and is perceived as being altruistic, but also denies being purely altruistic, even while acknowledging that she is making a sacrifice.[33]

A multivocal statement like this seems so effortless that the conditions making it possible can easily be missed. The fact of having had an exchange at a soup kitchen is less important than regarding the use of it as a legitimate response. The exchange substitutes for taking a single position on whether one is individualistic or altruistic. It depends on a certain level of flexibility or even decoupling of the various components of one's self—what psychologist Kenneth J. Gergen calls *multiphrenia* or the "splitting of the individual into a multiplicity of self-investments."[34] A multiphrenic person does not say, as Martin Luther did, "Here I stand. I can do no other." Instead, there is a separation of roles and of facets of the self to the point that one can imagine taking several different positions on a topic and engaging in a kind of internal conversation among the proponents of those views. It becomes possible to say, "I heard that Albert Einstein thought it was possible to believe in God and be a scientist, so I suppose if I thought about it more, I might come to the same conclusion, although you could probably persuade me otherwise if we talked long enough." In this respect, multiphrenia means not only being able to see different sides of an argument but also being incapable of arriving at a firm judgment of one's own.

Real-life examples of multivocality in dealing with questions about science and religion are not hard to find. On October 24, 2005, the U.S. District Court transcript in *Kitzmiller v. Dover Area School District*—the much publicized case in which plaintiffs sued the Dover, Pennsylvania, school board for requiring that criticisms of evolution based on ideas about intelligent design be incorporated into the curriculum—included the following exchange between the plaintiffs' attorney Witold J. Walczak and Professor Stephen Fuller, a sociologist testifying as an expert witness on behalf of the defense:

> Q. Mr. Rothschild asked you, A theory is not going to graduate into a fact; right? And the answer was, Right, exactly, exactly. No, I mean, I do think there is—that the tone of the statement is a little confusing. I mean, so I'm agreeing with Miller [another witness] on that point.
> A. But what I'm agreeing with Miller on is, I can understand why he sort of sees it that way. I wasn't necessarily saying that I had some definitive view about what the statement meant, but rather that I was sympathetic to—you know, I could see where he was coming from in finding this problematic.

Although the attorney persisted in attempting to determine whether Fuller regarded evolution as theory, fact, or
some combination of the two, Fuller continued to insist
that he was merely thinking through the issue and could
see it from several different angles.[35]

A dispersed self that incorporates different voices
provides a discursive mechanism for reconciling religion
and science; in addition, the normative emphasis in our
society on tolerance provides a strong warrant for doing
so. Alan Wolfe, in *One Nation, After All,* argues that
middle-class Americans are remarkably generous toward
others who may have profound differences of belief—so
generous, in fact, that they are likely to say, "Oh neat,
that's a cool view. I'm glad you said that."[36] Wolfe's argument is especially relevant to the question of conflict between religion and science because he concludes that the
so-called culture war, which pits fundamentalists against
those with more enlightened views, does not characterize
the majority of Americans.[37] Instead, the prevailing view
is that we may have our differences but should abide by
the law and treat all views with respect. Wolfe has been
interpreted as suggesting that America consists largely of
a muddled middle, flanked by extremists on the right and
left. That rendering, though, misses the subtlety of middle American culture. Not only are diverse opinions tol-
erated; there is also a kind of tentativeness, even cynicism,
about truth. A person has difficulty holding fast to a
conviction because it is no longer possible to know what
is true.[38]

If this argument is correct, the both-and position on
science and religion is less a statement about how the
two are complementary and more a way of expressing

uncertainty about what either claims to provide. For instance, in arguing that science describes nature while religion deals with questions of meaning and value, a person can in effect point to the limitations of both. Descriptions of nature are incomplete, disappointing, even meaningless, and yet the big questions that religion tries to answer may also be elusive. Thus, concerns about the hubris of science do not take shape as convictions about religion but as unanswered questions about the worth of scientific knowledge. Similarly, doubts about religion remain as uncertainties rather than translating into a devout faith in science.

In all of this, understandings of religion and science necessarily change. Both become more highly personalized, although in different ways. When people associate religion with why questions, words, the supernatural, and the spiritual, they do not mean that the biblical account of creation should be taken literally or that Vatican teachings about God are authoritative. They mean instead that religion helps them find meaning in life, gives them words to utter when they are despondent, and connects them with some larger dimension of life than the one they experience with their senses. Spirituality is not so much expressed in a creedal statement handed down from theologians but their view about what they might imagine the sacred to be like. Spirituality can thus remain popular in circles where participation in organized religion has become infrequent. For instance, in the survey showing hardly any scientists attending worship services, two-thirds nevertheless said they were spiritual and more than a third regarded themselves as very or moderately spiritual.[39]

The personalization of spirituality is associated with

broader characteristics of American religion that I have described as a kind of grassroots theology involving autobiographical narratives that emphasize spiritual journeys, tinkering, and negotiation.[40] Spiritual seekers are not uncommitted to their quest for the sacred; indeed, they often take it quite seriously. They nevertheless find answers in multiple venues, picking and choosing what they consider personally meaningful rather than feeling a need to accept entire traditions or universal truths.

Two other features of contemporary understandings of religion contribute to the ease with which many Americans reconcile it with science. One is the idea that God is ultimately a mystery, meaning that all teachings about God are at best flawed or incapable of authoritative interpretations. This view diminishes the significance of creeds and amplifies the importance of personal experience. It permits believing that God created the universe without implying that one knows how this may have happened or even what exactly that divine force may have been. The other is that the meaning of sacred texts necessarily changes as well. Although the Bible may be regarded as a source of divine truth, its words are less likely to be accepted as literal truth, and even among those who do regard it this way, the idea that it is free of errors becomes less important than the fact that it is a source of guidance and comfort.

Being able to relativize arguments by defining their significance strictly in personal terms sometimes occurs when people talk about science as well. A thoughtful young man named Steve who participated in a recent national study of teenagers, for example, worried that evolution emphasizes self-preservation, which in turn could conflict with universalistic religious notions of morality; he did not worry very deeply about this potential conflict, though, because the ideas were just "fun to think about and kind of interesting, 'cause, I don't know, I don't really let it bother me." He tempers his views about morality and rationality by asserting, "let each person decide for themselves."[41]

Personalization in science more often takes a different form than it does in religion, however. It is less a matter of assuming that science consists of private beliefs than of believing that its purpose is to bless us with personal goods. In a survey conducted for the National Science Foundation, for instance, 86 percent of Americans agreed that "science and technology are making our lives healthier, easier, and more comfortable."[42] Science is in this sense pragmatic. From day to day, it matters less whether science reveals how life evolved than that it yields vaccines and new pharmaceuticals. Knowing that humans share a high proportion of genetic material with other primates is a matter of idle curiosity. It is a thought we are willing to entertain as long as genetic research provides answers to riddles about birth defects and disease.

The Cultural Challenge

To conclude then: Laments about the continuing conflicts between science and religion, I have suggested, are less interesting than the fact that most people perceive no contradictions between the two. To be sure, many find it worrisome when fundamentalists seek to define religious arguments as science and people thus consider it laudable when theologians and scientists engage each other in dialogue. However, the value of such dialogue does not lie in eradicating the historic grounds on which the battles between religion and science have been fought. It lies instead in delineating more thoughtfully what each has to offer and how each may influence the other. Interaction of this kind requires scientists and religious leaders to speak beyond their own disciplines and in ways that engage the wider public.

Thoughtful discussions of the relationships between religion and science remain rare. Critics of intelligent design and creationism warn appropriately that science classes are not the place for these religious ideas to be introduced. Yet separation of church and state generally discourages schools from including religion in other parts of the curriculum. Meanwhile, religious congregations are unlikely venues for informed discussion because of inadequate time, interest, or training in science. Television commentary and newspaper editorials thus become one of the few places in which questions about the relationships between science and religion appear.

The reason these discussions are difficult is not because the public is caught up in bitter disputes about what should be taught in science classes but because the both-and view of science and religion has become all too familiar. When the culture tells us that all reasonable possibilities can easily be reconciled, it is time to take another look. Religion reduced to personal opinion is diminished nearly beyond recognition, just as science is when creature comforts become the sole reason for studying and supporting it. Distasteful as those school board debates may be, we might give them some credit for articulating contradictions too readily denied.

Notes

Introduction

1. David Hume, *Dialogues Concerning Natural Religion,* ed. Martin Bell (London: Penguin Classics, 1990), 38.

2. John Hedley Brooke, *Science and Religion: Some Historical Perspectives* (Cambridge: Cambridge University Press, 1991).

3. I have commented elsewhere about being quoted out of context so that my statements about evolutionary biology were made to seem like a disavowal. Keith Thomson, "Hooke, Fossils, and the Anti-evolutionists," *American Scientist* 91 (2003): 210–12.

4. Charles Darwin, *Autobiography,* ed. Michael Neve (London: Penguin Classics, 2002), 53.

5. Keith Thomson, *Before Darwin: Reconciling God and Science* (New Haven: Yale University Press, 2005).

6. Kenneth R. Miller, "Falling over the Edge," *Nature* 447 (2007): 1055–56.

7. In a sense, Hume failed: *Dialogues* could not be published in his lifetime.

8. Steven Prothero, *Religious Literacy: What Every American Needs to Know—but Doesn't* (San Francisco: Harper Collins, 2007).

9. In 1998 Richard W. Riley, then U.S. Secretary of Education, sent to schools a circular entitled *Presidential Guidelines, Religious Expression in Public Schools.* Among its many sections, it stated: "Public schools may not provide religious instruction, but they may teach *about* religion, including the Bible or other scripture: the history of religion, comparative religion, the Bible (or other

scripture)-as-literature, and the role of religion in the history of the United States and other countries all are permissible public school subjects. Similarly, it is permissible to consider religious influences on art, music, literature, and social studies. Although public schools may teach about religious holidays, including their religious aspects, and may celebrate the secular aspects of holidays, schools may not observe holidays as religious events or promote such observance by students." Amen to that.

RONALD L. NUMBERS,
"Aggressors, Victims, and Peacemakers"

1. Isaac Newton, *The Mathematical Principles of Natural Philosophy* (New York: Daniel Adee, 1848; first published, in Latin, in 1687), 506. The occasional exception is a literary expression from Francis Bacon's *Advancement of Learning,* where he alludes to "the two clear eyes of religion and natural philosophy." See, e.g., "Readings from Lord Bacon. No. 2," *Southern Literary Messenger* 16 (1850): 267–71; "Questions, Answers, &c.," *New York Observer and Chronicle* 34 (1856): 205. References to "faith and reason" were not uncommon, but they typically appeared in discussions of the bases for religious belief, not knowledge of nature. See especially John Locke, *An Essay Concerning Human Understanding,* Book IV, Chap. 18, "Of Faith and Reason, and Their Distinct Provinces." My generalizations are based exclusively on English-language sources.

2. Samuel Miller, *A Brief Retrospect of the Eighteenth Century,* 2 vols. (New York: T. and J. Swords, 1803), 2:233–34.

3. Peter Harrison, " 'Science' and 'Religion': Constructing the Boundaries," *Journal of Religion* 86 (2006): 81–106. See also Peter Harrison, *"Religion" and the Religions in the English Enlightenment* (Cambridge: Cambridge University Press, 1990); and James Moore, "Religion and Science," in *The Cambridge History of Science,* vol. 6, ed. Peter Bowler and John Pickstone (Cambridge: Cambridge University Press, in press).

4. Georges Louis Leclerc, comte de Buffon, *Natural History:*

General and Particular, trans. William Smellie, 7 vols. (London: W. Strahan & T. Cadell, 1781), 1:34, 63–82; Ronald L. Numbers, *Creation by Natural Law: Laplace's Nebular Hypothesis in American Thought* (Seattle: University of Washington Press, 1977), 6–8. On Buffon's religious beliefs, see Jacques Roger, *Buffon: A Life in Natural History*, trans. Sarah Lucille Bonnefoi, ed. L. Pearce Williams (Ithaca, N.Y.: Cornell University Press, 1997), 431.

5. Review of *A Treatise on the Plague and Yellow Fever*, by James Tytler, *Medical Repository* 3 (1800): 373–79, quotation on p. 376; Benjamin Silliman, "Address before the Association of American Geologists and Naturalists, Assembled at Boston, April 24, 1842," *American Journal of Science* 43 (1842): 217–50, quotation on p. 218. For a history of methodological naturalism, see Ronald L. Numbers, "Science Without God: Natural Laws and Christian Beliefs," in *When Science and Christianity Meet*, ed. David C. Lindberg and Ronald L. Numbers (Chicago: University of Chicago Press, 2003), 265–85.

6. [James Read Eckard], "The Logical Relations of Religion and Natural Science," *Biblical Repertory and Princeton Review* 32 (1860): 577–608, especially p. 577 (atheistic). For similar complaints about the naturalization of science, see William D. Whitney, "Is the Study of Language a Physical Science?" *North American Review* 101 (1865): 434–74; and [C. A. Aiken], "Whitney on Language," *Princeton Review* 40 (1868): 263–92, quotation on p. 270 (incredulous). I am indebted to Jon Roberts for identifying Eckard and to Steve Alter for identifying Aiken.

7. William Paley, *Natural Theology; or, Evidences of the Existence and Attributes of the Deity, Collected from the Appearances of Nature* (New York: Evert Duyckinck; first published in 1802), 42. On doxological literature, see Theodore Dwight Bozeman, *Protestants in an Age of Science: The Baconian Ideal and Antebellum American Religious Thought* (Chapel Hill: University of North Carolina Press, 1977).

8. Edward Hitchcock, *Religion of Geology and Its Connected Sciences* (Boston: Phillips, Sampson, 1854; first published in 1851), 474, 476. On natural theology in America, see E. Brooks Holifield,

Theology in America: Christian Thought from the Age of the Puritans to the Civil War (New Haven: Yale University Press, 2003), 180–86.

9. Walter H. Conser, Jr., *God and the Natural World: Religion and Science in Antebellum America* (Columbia: University of South Carolina Press, 1993), 9 (Hitchcock); A[lexander] Winchell, *Creation: The Work of One Intelligence, and Not the Product of Physical Forces* (Ann Arbor, Mich.: Young Men's Literary Assn., 1858), 3; Neal C. Gillespie, "Preparing for Darwin: Conchology and Natural Theology in Anglo-American Natural History," *Studies in History of Biology* 7 (1984): 93–145, especially 94–95.

10. E. Brooks Holifield, "Science and Theology in the Old South," in *Science and Medicine in the Old South*, ed. Ronald L. Numbers and Todd L. Savitt (Baton Rouge: Louisiana State University Press, 1989), 127–46, quotation on 127.

11. Numbers, *Creation by Natural Law*, 89.

12. Robert Bakewell, *An Introduction to Geology*, ed. B. Silliman, 2nd American from the 4th London ed. (New Haven, Conn.: Hezekiah Howe, 1833), 389–466, quotation on 461. On the English context for Silliman's views, see Nicolaas A. Rupke, *The Great Chain of History: William Buckland and the English School of Geology, 1814–1849* (Oxford: Oxford University Press, 1983).

13. Francis C. Haber, *The Age of the World: Moses to Darwin* (Baltimore: Johns Hopkins University Press, 1959), 259–63.

14. Nathan Reingold, ed., *The Papers of Joseph Henry*, vol. 2 (Washington, D.C.: Smithsonian Institution Press, 1975), 134–37 (infidel, Bible); Thomas Cooper, *On the Connection between Geology and the Pentateuch: In a Letter to Professor Silliman* (Columbia: Privately printed, 1833), unpaginated preface (garb), 58 (intermingle), 63 (intermeddling), 61–62 (surrender). On Silliman, see also Chandos Michael Brown, *Benjamin Silliman: A Life in the Young Republic* (Princeton, N.J.: Princeton University Press, 1989). On Cooper, see also Dumas Malone, *The Public Life of Thomas Cooper, 1783–1839* (New Haven: Yale University Press, 1926).

15. Philip J. Lawrence, "Edward Hitchcock: The Christian Geologist," *Proceedings of the American Philosophical Society* 116

(1972): 21–34, especially p. 28 (Stuart); Brown, *Benjamin Silliman*, 111–12 (Silliman); John H. Giltner, *Moses Stuart: The Father of Biblical Science in America* (Atlanta: Scholars Press, 1988), 7 (languages), 9 (higher criticism), 66–69 (Genesis and geology), 73 (digging of rocks). The best discussion of Genesis and geology in America is Rodney Lee Stiling, "The Diminishing Deluge: Noah's Flood in Nineteenth-Century American Thought," Ph.D. dissertation, University of Wisconsin–Madison, 1991. On Stuart, see also Jerry Wayne Brown, *The Rise of Biblical Criticism in America, 1800–1870: The New England Scholars* (Middletown, Conn.: Wesleyan University Press, 1969), 101–2.

16. The classic account of this tension is James R. Moore, "Geologists and Interpreters of Genesis in the Nineteenth Century," in *God and Nature: A History of the Encounter between Christianity and Science,* ed. David C. Lindberg and Ronald L. Numbers (Berkeley: University of California Press, 1986), 322–50.

17. Ronald L. Numbers, "Charles Hodge and the Beauties and Deformities of Science," in *Charles Hodge Revisited: A Critical Appraisal of His Life and Work,* ed. John W. Stewart and James H. Moorhead (Grand Rapids, Mich.: Wm. B. Eerdmans, 2002), 77–101, from which this account is extracted. See also Alexander A. Hodge, *The Life of Charles Hodge, D.D., LL.D.* (London: T. Nelson and Sons, 1881); and John W. Stewart, "Mediating the Center: Charles Hodge on American Science, Language, Literature, and Politics," *Studies in Reformed Theology and History* 3 (Winter 1995): 1–114.

18. William Stanton, *The Leopard's Spots: Scientific Attitudes Toward Race in America, 1815–59* (Chicago: University of Chicago Press, 1960), 25–35 (Morton). On the history of polygenism, see also G. Blair Nelson, " 'Men before Adam!': American Debates over the Unity and Antiquity of Humanity," in *When Science and Christianity Meet,* ed. Lindberg and Numbers, 161–81; and David N. Livingstone, *Adam's Ancestors: Race, Religion, and the Politics of Human Origins* (Baltimore: Johns Hopkins University Press, 2008).

19. Stanton, *Leopard's Spots,* 68 (human knowledge); Reginald Horsman, *Josiah Nott of Mobile: Southerner, Physician, and Racial*

Theorist (Baton Rouge: Louisiana State University Press, 1987), 170–221; Bruce Dain, *A Hideous Monster of the Mind: American Race Theory in the Early Republic* (Cambridge, Mass.: Harvard University Press, 2002), 221 (last great battle). See also Edward Lurie, *Louis Agassiz: A Life in Science* (Chicago: University of Chicago Press, 1960), 256–65.

20. Review of *The Races of Men*, by Robert Knox, *Biblical Repertory and Princeton Review* 23 (1851): 168–71, quotation on p. 171 (fought upon this field); Numbers, "Charles Hodge," 93–96. See also Lester D. Stephens, *Science, Race, and Religion in the American South: John Bachman and the Charleston Circle of Naturalists, 1815–1895* (Chapel Hill: University of North Carolina Press, 2000).

21. Numbers, *Creation by Natural Law*, 28–35, quotations on 32 (atheism, rabid tirade); James A. Secord, *Victorian Sensation: The Extraordinary Publication, Reception, and Secret Authorship of* Vestiges of the Natural History of Creation (Chicago: University of Chicago Press, 2000), 6 (evolutionary vision); [Edward Strong], "Vestiges of Creation and Its Reviewers," *New Englander* 4 (1846): 113–27, quotation on p. 115 (annihilates religion).

22. [George Frederick Holmes], "Philosophy and Faith," *Methodist Quarterly Review* 3 (1851): 185–218, quotation on p. 186; Jon H. Roberts, *Darwinism and the Divine in America: Protestant Intellectuals and Organic Evolution, 1859–1900* (Madison: University of Wisconsin Press, 1988), 64 (Armageddon).

23. Charles Darwin, *The Descent of Man, and Selection in Relation to Sex*, 2 vols. (New York: D. Appleton, 1871), 1: 147 (overthrow), 2:372 (quadruped); Ronald L. Numbers, *Darwinism Comes to America* (Cambridge, Mass.: Harvard University Press, 1998), 31 (earthquake).

24. Numbers, *Darwinism Comes to America*, 27 (Gray); William Paley, *Natural Theology; or, Evidences of the Existence and Attributes of the Deity, Collected from the Appearances of Nature* (London: J. Faulder, 1802), 26 (cure for atheism); Charles Darwin, *On the Origin of Species by Means of Natural Selection* (London: John Murray, 1859), 186–88; Asa Gray to Charles Darwin, January 23, 1860, in *The Correspondence of Charles Darwin*, vol. 8:

1860 (Cambridge: Cambridge University Press, 1993), 47 (weakest part); Charles Darwin to Asa Gray, February 8 or 9, 1860, ibid., p. 75 (shudder). On Gray, see A. Hunter Dupree, *Asa Gray, 1810–1888* (Cambridge, Mass.: Harvard University Press, 1959).

25. Charles Darwin, *The Variation of Animals and Plants under Domestication*, 2 vols., 2nd ed. (New York: D. Appleton, 1883; first published in 1868), 2:428; Roberts, *Darwinism and the Divine in America*, 80; Numbers, "Charles Hodge," 97–100. [See the essay in this collection by Alvin Plantinga for a contemporary attempt to defend a view of "guided evolution." Ed.]

26. A. S. Gardiner, "Religion and Science," *New York Evangelist* 48 (21 June 1877): 2 (truce); Numbers, *Darwinism Comes to America*, 42 (Morse); Roberts, *Darwinism and the Divine in America*, 230 (danger).

27. Andrew Dickson White, "The Battle-Fields of Science," *New-York Daily Tribune*, December 18, 1869, 4. Much of this paragraph is taken from David C. Lindberg and Ronald L. Numbers, "Beyond War and Peace: A Reappraisal of the Encounter Between Christianity and Science," *Church History* 55 (1986): 338–54. Still the best critique of the warfare thesis is James R. Moore, *The Post-Darwinian Controversies: A Study of the Protestant Struggle to Come to Terms with Darwin in Great Britain and America, 1870–1900* (Cambridge: Cambridge University Press, 1979), 19–122.

28. "The Book of the Wars of the Lord," *Outlook* 53 (1896): 1153; Andrew D. White, Letter to the Editor, *Boston Medical and Surgical Journal* 125 (1891): 204–7 (TRUTH).

29. Moore, *Post-Darwinian Controversies*, 28 (popularity); review of *History of the Conflict Between Science and Religion*, by John William Draper, *Universalist Quarterly and General Review* 12 (1875): 251–53 (the question); "Draper's Conflict Between Religion and Science," *Catholic World* 21 (1875): 178–200, quotation on p. 179 (farrago); Orestes Brownson, review of *History of the Conflict between Science and Religion*, by John William Draper, *Brownson's Quarterly Review* 3 (1875): 153–73, especially 156 (coarse and vulgar), 166–67 (real offense), 169 (highway-robberies). On Draper, see also Donald Fleming, *John William*

Draper and the Religion of Science (Philadelphia: University of Pennsylvania Press, 1950).

30. Frank M. Turner, *Between Science and Religion: The Reaction to Scientific Naturalism in Late Victorian England* (New Haven: Yale University Press, 1974), 16 (secularization). See also Frank M. Turner, *Contesting Cultural Authority: Essays in Victorian Intellectual Life* (Cambridge: Cambridge University Press, 1993); and Bernard Lightman, *The Origins of Agnosticism: Victorian Unbelief and the Limits of Knowledge* (Baltimore: Johns Hopkins University Press, 1987).

31. [Thomas H. Huxley], "Science and Religion," *The Builder* 17 (January 1859): 35–36; Adrian Desmond, *Huxley: From Devil's Disciple to Evolution's High Priest* (Reading, Mass.: Addison-Wesley, 1997), 253 (Parsondom), 630 (omniscience); Thomas H. Huxley, *Darwiniana: Essays* (New York: D. Appleton, 1894), 52 (Hercules), in an essay first published in 1860; G. Frederick Wright, "Huxley Among the False Prophets," *Advance* 23 (1889): 452 (every parish).

32. Roberts, *Darwinism and the Divine in America*, 74 (boldest challenge); John Tyndall, *Fragments of Science*, 6th ed. (New York: D. Appleton, 1889), 472–534, especially 524 (promise and potency), 525 (materialism), 530 (entire domain). For Tyndall's subsequent clarifications, see pp. 541 (Middle Ages), 544 (unjustifiable raid), 545 (permanent peace), and 546 (storm of opprobrium). On the prayer test, see Frank M. Turner, "Rainfall, Plagues, and the Prince of Wales: A Chapter in the Conflict of Science and Religion," *Journal of British Studies* 13 (1973): 46–65; and Robert Bruce Mullin, "Science, Miracles, and the Prayer-Gauge Debate," in *When Science and Christianity Meet*, ed. Lindberg and Numbers, 203–24.

33. W. E. Gladstone, *The Impregnable Rock of Holy Scripture* (Philadelphia: John D. Wattles, 1891), 311 (advancing forces); David Bebbington, *The Mind of Gladstone: Religion, Homer, and Politics* (Oxford: Oxford University Press, 2004), 234–36 ("Science"); W. E. Gladstone, T. H. Huxley, and Others, *The Order of Creation: The Conflict Between Genesis and Geology* (New York:

Truth Seeker, n.d.), 58 (Sisyphus), 60 (ignorance), 63 (heathen survivals), 70 (unmeasured scorn); R. W., "Huxley's Latest 'Science
and Christian Theology,'" *Methodist Review* 3 (1887): 778–80
(churchmen).

34. [Lemuel Moss], "Present Relation of Scientific Thought to
Christianity," *Baptist Quarterly Review* 4 (1882): 1–35, quotation
from Princeton scientist on p. 30; George M Beard, "The Boston
Monday Lectureship," *Independent* 28 (February 1, 1877): 1.

35. Duke of Argyll, *The Reign of Law* (New York: George
Routledge & Sons, 1872; first published in 1867); Mary Lesley
Ames, ed., *Life and Letters of Peter and Susan Lesley*, 2 vols. (New
York: G. P. Putnam's Sons, 1909), 2:347–48 (humbug).

36. Ronald L. Numbers, *The Creationists: From Scientific Creationism to Intelligent Design*, expanded ed. (Cambridge, Mass.:
Harvard University Press, 2006), 51 (invaded his realm), 89 (*Science*), 103 (does away with God); Numbers, *Darwinism Comes to
America*, 117 (Satan). On the "scientism" of Huxley and Tyndall,
see, e.g., "Mivart's 'Lessons from Nature,'" *Catholic World* 24
(1876): 1–13.

37. Numbers, *The Creationists*, pp. 53 (Mathews), 61 (Adam
and Eve); H. L. Mencken, "Battle Now Over, Mencken Sees; Genesis Triumphant and Ready for New Jousts," *Baltimore Evening
Sun*, July 18, 1925. Matthews edited a series of "Popular Religious
Leaflets" on harmonizing "Science and Religion," which rivaled
the conservative *Fundamentals* in circulation though not in recognition; see Edward B. Davis, "Science and Religious Fundamentalism in the 1920s," *American Scientist* 93 (2005): 253–60.

38. Numbers, *The Creationists*, 65. On the legal debates over
the teaching of evolution, see Edward J. Larson, *Trial and Error:
The American Controversy over Creation and Evolution* (New
York: Oxford University Press, 1985).

39. Larson, *Trial and Error*, 181–84; James Gilbert, *Redeeming
Culture: American Religion in an Age of Science* (Chicago: University of Chicago Press, 1997), 121–45 (Moody), 273–95 (IRAS).

40. Larson, *Trial and Error*, 86 (slogan); Numbers, *The Creationists*, 264–65 (creationist reactions).

41. Numbers, *The Creationists*, 278–79; Langdon Gilkey, *Creationism on Trial: Evolution and God at Little Rock* (Minneapolis: Winston Press, 1985), 169.

42. Phillip E. Johnson, *Darwin on Trial* (Downers Grove, Ill.: InterVarsity Press, 1991); Larry Vardiman, "Scientific Naturalism as Science," *Impact* #293, an unpaginated insert in *Acts & Facts*, 26 (November 1997) (reclaiming science). This account of ID is based on Numbers, *The Creationists*, 373–98. For a critique of methodological naturalism, see Phillip E. Johnson, Foreword, in *The Creation Hypothesis: Scientific Evidence for an Intelligent Designer*, ed. J. P. Moreland (Downers Grove, Ill.: InterVarsity Press, 1994), 7–8. Ironically, the phrase "methodological naturalism" had been coined by an evangelical Christian in the early 1980s to describe a conciliatory stance for Christian scientists to take; see Numbers, *The Creationists*, 376–77.

43. Michael J. Behe, *Darwin's Black Box: The Biochemical Challenge to Evolution* (New York: Free Press, 1996), 15, 33, 193, 232–33 (Newton et al.); "The Evolution of a Skeptic: An Interview with Dr. Michael Behe, Biochemist and Author of Recent Best-Seller *Darwin's Black Box*," *The Real Issue* 15 (November/December 1996): 1, 6–8. For a historical overview of the intelligent design movement, on which this account is largely based, see Numbers, *The Creationists*, 373–98.

44. Darwin, *Descent of Man*, 1:4.

45. [See Alvin Plantinga's essay in this collection. Ed.]

46. Alvin Plantinga, "Methodological Naturalism?" *Perspectives on Science and Christian Faith* 49 (September 1997): 143–54; Phil Cousineau, ed., *The Way Things Are: Conversations with Huston Smith on the Spiritual Life* (Berkeley: University of California Press, 2003), 135–36, 150–51; David K. Webb, Letter to the Editor, *Origins and Design* 17 (Spring 1996): 5 (bullshit); Noam Chomsky, "Evolution, Ecology and 'Malignant Design,'" *Toronto Star*, November 14, 2005, at www.commondreams.org; J. W. Haas, Jr., "On Intelligent Design, Irreducible Complexity, and Theistic Science," *Perspectives on Science and Christian Faith* 49 (March 1997): 1.

47. Richard Dawkins, *The Blind Watchmaker* (New York:

W. W. Norton, 1986), 5–6 (intellectually fulfilled), 316; Dawkins, review of *Blueprints: Solving the Mystery of Evolution*, by Maitland A. Edey and Donald C. Johanson, *New York Times*, April 9, 1989, section 7, p. 34 (ignorant); Dawkins, "Is Science a Religion?" *The Humanist* 57 (January/February 1997): 26–29, quotation on p. 26; Alister McGrath, *Dawkins' God: Genes, Memes, and the Meaning of Life* (Oxford: Blackwell, 2005), 84 (mental illness and cop-out); Richard Dawkins, *The God Delusion* (Boston: Houghton Mifflin, 2006), 66–69; Roger Downey, "Darwin's Watchdog," *Eastsideweek*, December 11, 1996 (Rottweiler).

48. Owen Gingerich, *God's Universe* (Cambridge, Mass.: Harvard University Press, 2006), p. 74 (single-handedly); Madeleine Bunting, "Why the Intelligent Design Lobby Thanks God for Richard Dawkins," *Guardian*, March 27, 2006, at www.guard ian.co.uk.

49. Daniel C. Dennett, *Darwin's Dangerous Idea: Evolution and the Meaning of Life* (New York: Simon and Schuster, 1995), 515–16, 519–21. See also Dennett, "Appraising Grace: What Evolutionary Good Is God?" *The Sciences* 37 (January/February 1997): 39–44.

50. Francis Crick, quoted in Margaret Wertheim, "After the Double Helix: Unraveling the Mysteries of the State of Being," *New York Times*, April 13, 2004, p. D3; Peter Atkins, *Galileo's Finger: The Ten Great Ideas of Science* (Oxford: Oxford University Press, 2003), 237; Edward O. Wilson, *On Human Nature* (1978), 188, 192; William B. Provine, *Origins Research* 16 (no. 1, 1994): 9; Carl Sagan, *Cosmos* (New York: Ballantine Books, 1985), 1, based on the television series, which first aired in 1980.

51. Stephen Jay Gould, *Rocks of Ages: Science and Religion in the Fullness of Life* (New York: Ballantine, 1999), 4 (goodwill, science, religion), 6 (magisterial), 209 (discouraged).

52. Allan C. Hutchinson, "Darwin's Cocker-Spaniel," (Toronto) *Globe and Mail*, September 2, 2006, available at www.the globeandmail.com; Michael Ruse, *Can a Darwinian Be a Christian? The Relationship Between Science and Religion* (Cambridge: Cambridge University Press, 2001), 217; Ruse, *The Evolution-Creation Struggle* (Cambridge, Mass.: Harvard University Press,

2005), 4 (evolutionism), 201 (secular religion); Michael Ruse, "Fighting the Fundamentalists: Chamberlain or Churchill?" *Skeptical Inquirer* 31 (March/April 2007): 38–41. On Dawkins, see also Karl Giberson and Mariano Artigas, *Oracles of Science: Celebrity Scientists Versus God and Reason* (Oxford: Oxford University Press, 2007), chap. 1, "A Good Devil's Chaplain."

53. Peter Dizikes, "Evolutionary War," *Boston Globe*, May 1, 2005 (very difficult); William Dembski, "Remarkable Exchange Between Michael Ruse and Daniel Dennett," February 21, 2006, at www.uncommondescent.com.

54. Jonathan Wells, *The Politically Incorrect Guide to Darwinism and Intelligent Design* (Washington, D.C.: Regnery, 2006), 175 (surrender); Jerry Coyne, "Intergalactic Jesus," *London Review of Books*, May 9, 2002, 23–24 (end of careers); Dawkins, *The God Delusion*, 66–69 (Chamberlain); Dembski, "Remarkable Exchange" (forces of darkness). See also Jerry Coyne, "The Faith That Dare Not Speak Its Name: The Case Against Intelligent Design," *New Republic*, August 22 and 29, 2005, 21–33; Richard Dawkins and Jerry Coyne, "One Side Can Be Wrong," *Guardian*, September 1, 2005, at www.guardian.co.uk; and Richard Dawkins, "Why There Almost Certainly Is No God," *Huffington Post*, October 23, 2006, at www.huffingtonpost.com.

55. Numbers, *The Creationists*, chap. 18, "Creationism Goes Global." I am indebted to Charles Cohen for the phrase "irreconcilable epistemologies." On the continuing religiosity of scientists, see, e.g., Edward J. Larson and Larry Witham, "Scientists and Religion in America," *Scientific American* 281 (September 1999): 88–89, which revealed that nearly 40 percent of the scientists polled professed belief in a personal god "to whom one may pray in expectation of receiving an answer" and who has the power to grant immortality. It seems highly likely that more than 10 percent believed in a less robust god.

56. Ann Coulter, *Godless: The Church of Liberalism* (New York: Crown Forum, 2006), 246 (rhetoric). On ID's public-relations campaign, see Numbers, *The Creationists*, 396–97. On journalistic "balance," see Chris Mooney, "Blinded by Science: How 'Balanced' Coverage Lets the Scientific Fringe Hijack Real-

ity," *Columbia Journalism Review* 43 (November/December 2004): 26–35; and Chris Mooney and Matthew C. Nisbet, "Undoing Darwin," *Columbia Journalism Review* 44 (September/October 2005): 31–39. In 1999 the president of the International Council for Science estimated that there were "perhaps 3 to 10 million active scientists worldwide"; see Werner Arber, "World Conference on Science," *Science International,* September 1999, cover. I conservatively used three million in my calculation. George W. Gilchrist, "The Elusive Scientific Basis of Intelligent Design Theory," *NCSE Reports* 17 (May/June 1997): 14–15, reported that a search of approximately 6,000 journals in the life sciences indexed by BIOSIS and published between 1991 and 1997 turned up only one reference to intelligent design.

57. Ann Coulter, front-cover blurb on Jonathan Wells, *The Politically Incorrect Guide to Darwinism and Intelligent Design* (Washington, D.C.: Regnery, 2006); Charles Krauthammer, "Phony Theory, False Conflict: 'Intelligent Design' Foolishly Pits Evolution Against Faith," *Washington Post,* November 18, 2005, p. A23; Numbers, *The Creationists,* 394 (inanity); Michael R. Bloomberg, "Address to Graduates of Johns Hopkins University School of Medicine," May 25, 2006, quoted in Wells, *Politically Incorrect Guide,* 157; Coulter, *Godless,* 199 (Scientology). For Conservatives Against Intelligent Design, see www.caidweb.org.

58. "2004 Presidential Forum: Bush and Kerry Offer Their Views on Science," *Science* 306 (2004): 46–52; Elisabeth Bumiller, "Bush Remarks Roil Debate over Teaching of Evolution," *New York Times,* August 3, 2005, p. A15; David Stout, "Frist Urges 2 Teachings on Life Origin," *New York Times,* August 20, 2005, p. A12; Deborah Solomon, "Schoolwork: Questions for Margaret Spellings," *New York Times Magazine,* May 22, 2005, 19. On press coverage of the "controversy," see Chris Mooney and Matthew C. Nisbet, "Undoing Darwin," *Columbia Journalism Review* 44 (September/October 2005): 31–39.

59. Jeffrey M. Jones, "Most Americans Engaged in Debate About Evolution, Creation," October 13, 2005, available at Gallup Web site, www.gallup.com; David W. Moore, "Most Americans Tentative About Origin-of-Life Explanations," September 23,

2005, Gallup Web site, www.gallup.com (the figure of 65.5 percent appears in the profile for Question 30C, surveyed August 5–7, 2005); Claudia Wallis, "Faith and Healing," *Time*, June 24, 1996, 63; Numbers, *The Creationists*, chap. 18, "Creationism Goes Global."

KENNETH R. MILLER, *"Darwin, God, and Dover"*

1. [The history on the American scene is well documented in the contribution to this collection by Ronald Numbers. Ed.]

2. Pam Belluck, "Board for Kansas Deletes Evolution from Curriculum," *New York Times*, August 12, 1999.

3. Pam Belluck, "Evolution Foes Dealt a Defeat In Kansas Vote," *New York Times*, August 3, 2000.

4. M. Davey and R. Blumenthal, "Fight over Evolution Shifts in Kansas School Board Vote," *New York Times*, August 3, 2006.

5. Tom DeLay, remarks reported in *Congressional Record* 145 (June 16, 1999): H4366.

6. Lauri Lebo, "Dover Figures Deny Remarks on Creationism," *York (PA) Daily Record*, January 16, 2005.

7. Percival Davis and Dean H. Kenyon, *Of Pandas and People: The Central Question of Biological Origins* (Charles B. Thaxton, ed.; Plano, Tex.: The Foundation for Thought and Ethics, 1993).

8. William Dembski, "The Vise Strategy: Squeezing the Truth out of Darwinists," from his blog, "Uncommon Descent," May 11, 2005; http://www.uncommondescent.com/archives/59.

9. National Academy of Sciences, *Science and Creationism* (Washington, D.C.: National Academy Press, 1999), 14.

10. Philip D. Gingerich, Munir ul Haq, Iyad S. Zalmout, Intizar H. Khan, and M. Sadiq Malkani, "Origin of Whales from Early Artiodactyls: Hands and Feet of Eocene Protocetidae from Pakistan," *Science* 293 (2001): 2239–42.

11. J. G. M. Thewissen and Sunil Bajpai, "Whale Origins as a Poster Child for Macroevolution," *Bioscience* 51 (2001): 1037–1049.

12. Sirpa Nummela, J. G. M. Thewissen, Sunil Bajpai, S. Taseer

Hussain, and Kishor Kumar, "Eocene Evolution of Whale Hearing," *Nature* 430 (2004): 776–780.

13. Ibid.

14. Chimpanzee Sequencing and Analysis Consortium, "Initial Sequence of the Chimpanzee Genome and Comparison with the Human Genome," *Nature* 437 (2005): 69–87.

15. See LaDeana W. Hillier et al., "Generation and Annotation of the DNA Sequences of Human Chromosomes 2 and 4," *Nature* 434 (2005): 724–31.

16. Michael J. Behe, "The Challenge of Irreducible Complexity," *Natural History* 111 (April 2002): 74.

17. Michael J. Behe, *Darwin's Black Box: The Biochemical Challenge to Evolution* (New York: Free Press, 1996), 39.

18. Mark J. Pallen and Nicholas J. Matzke, "From the Origin of Species to the Origin of Bacterial Flagella," *Nature Reviews Microbiology* 4 (2006): 784–790.

19. *Kitzmiller v. Dover*, 400 F. Supp. 2d 707 (M.D. Pa. 2005), p. 76.

20. Behe, *Darwin's Black Box*.

21. Yong Jiang and Russsell F. Doolittle, "The Evolution of Vertebrate Blood Coagulation as Viewed from a Comparison of Puffer Fish and Sea Squirt Genomes," *Proceedings of the National Academy of Sciences* 100 (2003): 7527–32.

22. Behe, *Darwin's Black Box*.

23. *Kitzmiller v. Dover*, 78.

24. Stephen C. Meyer, "Intelligent Design Is Not Creationism," *The Telegraph*, January 28, 2006. http://www.telegraph.co.uk/opinion/main.jhtml?xml=/opinion/2006/01/28/do2803.xml.

25. Davis and Kenyon, *Of Pandas and People*.

26. Ibid., 99–100.

27. *Biology and Origins* (1987), 14–15.

28. *Kitzmiller v. Dover*, 30.

29. David L. Hull, "The God of the Galápagos," *Nature* 352 (1991): 485–86.

30. Ibid.

31. Richard Dawkins, *River out of Eden: A Darwinian View of Life* (New York: Harper Collins, 1995), 133.

32. Charles Darwin, *On the Origin of Species* (London: John Murray, 1859).

33. Rob Boston, "Missionary Man," *Church and State* (1999, April).

34. Madeleine Bunting, "Why the Intelligent Design Lobby Thanks God for Richard Dawkins," *Guardian Unlimited*, March 27, 2006. http://education.guardian.co.uk/schools/comment/story/0,,1740547,00.html.

35. Daniel Dennett, *Darwin's Dangerous Idea: Evolution and the Meanings of Life* (London: Penguin, 1995), 50.

36. Augustine, *The Literal Meaning of Genesis*, Ancient Christian Writers 41 (New York: Newman Press, 1982), bk. 1, chap. 19.

37. International Theological Commission (ITC), "Communion and Stewardship: Human Persons Created in the Image of God," *Report of the International Theological Commission*, 2004, para. 64; http://www.vatican.va/roman_curia/congregations/cfaith/cti_documents/rc_con_cfaith_doc_20040723_communion-stewardship_en.html.

38. Ibid., para. 69.

ALVIN PLANTINGA, *"Science and Religion"*

1. For the earlier stages of the conflict, see the essay in this collection by Ronald Numbers, particularly his comments on the work of John W. Draper, *History of the Conflict Between Religion and Science* (New York: D. Appleton and Co., 1874).

2. What Peter Unger calls "the scientiphicalism." Peter Unger, "Free Will and Scientiphicalism," *Philosophy and Phenomenological Research* 65, no. 1 (2002): 1–25. In his mind, as in mine, there is no intrinsic connection between science and the scientiphicalism.

3. Bas C. van Fraassen, *The Empirical Stance* (New Haven: Yale University Press, 2002).

4. Richard Rorty, review of *The Empirical Stance* by Bas van Fraassen, in *Notre Dame Philosophical Reviews* (Notre Dame, Ind., July 7, 2002).

5. Richard Rorty, *Philosophy and the Mirror of Nature* (Princeton, N.J.: Princeton University Press, 1979).

6. Richard Rorty, *Irony, Contingency and Solidarity* (Cambridge: Cambridge University Press), 109.

7. A phrase van Fraassen gets from the historian Catherine Wilson.

8. Quoted in Leon Kass, *Toward a More Natural Science: Biology and Human Affairs* (New York: Free Press, 1985), 250.

9. A tendency that, for what it is worth, has been confirmed by studies in evolutionary psychology: see, for example, Justin Barrett, "Exploring the Natural Foundations of Religion," *Trends in Cognitive Science* 4, no. 1 (2000): 29–34; and *Why Would Anyone Believe in God?* (Walnut Creek, Calif.: AltaMira, 2004); Pascal Boyer, *The Naturalness of Religious Ideas: A Cognitive Theory of Religion* (Berkeley: University of California Press, 1994); and Todd Tremlin, *Minds and Gods: The Cognitive Foundations of Religion* (Oxford: Oxford University Press, 2006).

10. Obviously we don't take ourselves *completely* out of the picture, in doing science: we continue to endorse *modus ponens* as opposed to affirming the consequent; we rely on logic, mathematics, perception, measurement, the idea that there has been a past, etc., all of which are characteristically human ways of proceeding. Other, more subtle ways in which our human proclivities enter into scientific inquiry are pointed out in detail in Del Ratzsch, "Humanness in Their Hearts: Where Science and Religion Fuse," in Michael Murray, ed., *The Believing Primate* (Oxford: Oxford University Press, forthcoming). And of course there can be controversy as to whether a given part of the human cognitive constitution *should* be bracketed in science: if theism is true, for example, it is far from obvious that methodological naturalism gives us the best shot at reaching the truth. See Alvin Plantinga, "Augustinian Christian Philosophy," *The Monist* 75, no. 3 (July 1992): 291–320; and Plantinga, "Methodological Naturalism?" in *Facets of Faith and Science*, vol. 1, ed. J. van der Meer (Lanham, Mass.: University Press of America, 1996).

11. "Obviously": if, as many theists have thought, God is a necessary being, the proposition that there is such a person as God is necessarily true and thus entailed (though not obviously entailed) by every proposition.

12. In general, see Stillman Drake, *Galileo* (New York: Hill and Wang, 1980).

13. See Richard Dawkins, *The Blind Watchmaker: Why the Evidence of Evolution Reveals a Universe Without Design* (London: W. W. Norton & Co., 1986); and *A Devil's Chaplain: Reflections on Hope, Lies, Science, and Love* (Boston: Houghton Mifflin, 2003); Daniel Dennett, *Darwin's Dangerous Idea: Evolution and the Meanings of Life* (New York: Simon & Schuster, 1985); and Phillip Johnson, *Darwin on Trial,* 2nd ed. (Downers Grove, Ill.: InterVarsity Press, 1993).

14. Darwin (1887), Letter from T. H. Huxley to Charles Darwin, November 23, 1859, in *The Life and Letters of Charles Darwin,* vol. 2 (London: John Murray, 1887), 232.

15. Stephen Jay Gould, "Evolution as Fact and Theory," in *Hen's Teeth and Horse's Toes* (New York: Norton, 1983).

16. Why not suppose that life has originated just once, so that we needn't all be cousins? This suggestion is occasionally made, but the more usual idea is that life originated just once—if only because of the astounding difficulty in seeing how it could have originated (by merely natural processes) at all.

17. See Stephen Jay Gould, "Evolution as Fact and Theory"; Douglas Futuyma, *Evolutionary Biology,* 2nd ed. (Sunderland, Mass.: Sinauer Associates, 1986); and George G. Simpson, *Tempo and Mode in Evolution,* Columbia Classics in Evolution Series (New York: Columbia University Press, 1984).

18. Dawkins, *The Blind Watchmaker,* 5.

19. Dennett, *Darwin's Dangerous Idea.*

20. Ibid., 50.

21. Ibid., 203.

22. Ibid., 59.

23. John Locke, *An Essay Concerning Human Understanding,* vol. 2, ed. A. C. Fraser (Mineola, N.Y.: Dover Publications, 1959), x, 10.

24. Dennett, *Darwin's Dangerous Idea,* 516.

25. Ibid., 519.

26. But what if they *do* insist on teaching these heresies to their children? (Baptists will be Baptists, after all.) Will we be obliged to

remove Baptist children from their parents' noxious influence? Should we put barbed wire around those zoos, maybe check to see if perhaps there is room for them in northern Siberia? Dennett and Richard Rorty come from opposite ends of the philosophical spectrum, but Dennett's views here nicely match Rorty's declaration that in the new liberal society, those who believe there is a "chief end of man," as in the Westminster Shorter Catechism, will have to be regarded as "insane" (and perhaps deprived of the vote and institutionalized pending recovery from the seizure?).

27. Dennett, *Darwin's Dangerous Idea*, 315 (Dennett's emphasis).

28. Of course many claim that there are features of the world such that at the moment there are not any plausible stories of that sort—see, e.g., Michael Behe's *Darwin's Black Box* (New York: Free Press, 1996). So perhaps the idea is that the theory of natural selection gives us reason to think such stories will be forthcoming, or would be forthcoming given sufficient time and resources.

29. See Michael Ruse, *The Evolution Creation Struggle* (Cambridge, Mass.: Harvard University Press, 2005).

30. Ernst Mayr, *Towards a New Philosophy of Biology: Observations of an Evolutionist* (Cambridge, Mass.: Harvard University Press, 1988), 99; see also Elliott Sober, *Philosophy of Biology* (Boulder, Colo.: Westview Press, 1993).

31. Ernst Mayr, *This Is Biology: The Science of the Living World* (Cambridge, Mass.: Harvard University Press, 1997); see also Sober, *Philosophy of Biology.*

32. Alexander Pruss, "Divine Creation and Evolution," unpublished.

33. Ibid., 9.

34. Ibid.

LAWRENCE M. KRAUSS, *"Religion vs. Science?"*

1. *Congressional Record* 145 (June 16, 1999): H4366.

2. According to the U.S. Department of Treasury's Web site, "The unfinished pyramid means that the United States will always grow, improve and build. In addition, the 'All-Seeing Eye' located

above the pyramid suggests the importance of divine guidance in favor of the American cause." See http://www.ustreas.gov/educa tion/faq/currency/portraits.shtml.

3. See Peter Baker and Peter Slevin, "Bush Remarks on 'Intelligent Design' Theory Fuel Debate," *Washington Post,* August 3, 2005, p. A01, http://www.washingtonpost.com/wp-dyn/content/article/2005/08/02/AR2005080201686.html.

4. According to the National Science Foundation, "Although K–12 science instructional practices have improved greatly in the past few years, many schools are still not providing the quality science education outlined in the National Science Educational Standards (NSES), even with the U.S. fully immersed in effects to meet the educational accountability requirements set forth by the Federal No Child Left Behind Act of 2001 (NCLB), which took effect in 2002." "America's Pressing Challenge—Building a Stronger Foundation," National Science Foundation Web site, February 2006, http://www.nsf.gov/statistics/nsb0602/. I have addressed this issue elsewhere. See "The Back Page," *APS News* 15, no. 4 (April 2006): 419.

5. Cf. Statement of Norman R. Augustine, Retired Chairman and Chief Executive Officer, Lockheed Martin Corporation, and Chair, Committee on Prospering in the Global Economy of the 21st Century, Committee on Science, Engineering, and Public Policy, Division on Policy and Global Affairs, the National Academies before the Committee on Science, U.S. House of Representatives, October 20, 2005. Available at the National Academies Web site, http://www7.nationalacademies.org/ocga/testi mony/Prospering_in_the_Global_Economy_of_the_21st_Century.asp.

6. Gallup survey, November 7–10, 2004; available at Gallup Web site, www.gallup.com. Frank Newport, "American Beliefs: Evolution vs. Bible's Explanation of Human Origins: Education, Church Attendance, Partisanship Related to Beliefs," March 8, 2006, http://www.gallup.com/poll/21811/American-Beliefs-Evo lution-vs-Bibles-Explanation-Human-Origins.aspx.

7. See National Science Foundation, *Science and Engineering Indicators 2006,* Chapter 7.

8. Cornelia Dean, "Evolution Opponent Is in Line for Schools Post," *New York Times,* May 19, 2007.

9. See, e.g., Cf. Michael J. Behe, *Darwin's Black Box: The Biochemical Challenge to Evolution* (New York: Touchstone, 1996), 39.

10. The essay by Ronald Numbers in this collection illustrates some of the passion that has been devoted to the issue.

11. See the organization's Web site under "The Problem," http://www.sciohio.org/main.htm.

12. The organization's Web site is http://www.discovery.org/csc.

13. The Center for the Renewal of Science and Culture is now called the Center for Science and Culture. See their Web site: http://www.discovery.org/csc/aboutCSC.php.

14. See http://www.antievolution.org/features/wedge.html.

15. Ibid. The sentence opens the introduction to the "Wedge Strategy."

16. Ibid.

17. Lawrence M. Krauss, "School Boards Want to 'Teach the Controversy.' What Controversy?" *New York Times,* May 17, 2005, http://www.nytimes.com/2005/05/17/science/17comm.html?scp=5&sq=&st=nyt.

18. Christoph Schönborn, "Finding Design in Nature," *New York Times,* July 7, 2005, http://www.nytimes.com/2005/07/07/opinion/07schonborn.html.

19. Cf. John Brockman, "How Do You Fed-Ex the Pope? A Talk with Lawrence Krauss," *Edge,* June 22, 2006; http://www.edge.org/3rd_culture/krauss06/krauss06.1_index.html.

20. This "retraction" has been surmised based on his statements made in a lecture given at St. Stephen's Cathedral in Vienna, reported by Reuters. See Lucy Sherriff, "Creationism and Evolution Can Co-Exist, Says Cardinal: Darwin Gets Thumbs-Up (Again) from the Catholic Church," *The Register,* October 5, 2005; http://www.theregister.co.uk/2005/10/05/creation_evolution. Yet, this information is contra "Creation and Evolution: To the Debate as It Stands," available at http://stephanscom.at/edw/katechesen/articles/2005/10/14/a9347/.

21. Of the many treatments of the Scopes trial, see Jeffrey P. Moran, *Scopes Trial: A Brief History with Documents* (New York: Palgrave, 2002); and Edward J. Larson, *Summer for the Gods: The Scopes Trial and America's Continuing Debate over Science and Religion* (Cambridge, Mass.: Harvard University Press, 1998).

22. To review these legal decisions, see (a) *Susan Epperson, et al., Appellants, v. Arkansas.* No. 7. Supreme Court of the United States. Argued October 16, 1968. Decided November 12, 1968; http://www .law.umkc.edu/faculty/projects/ftrials/conlaw/Epperso.htm; and (b) Edwards, *Governor of Louisiana, et al., v. Aguillard, et al.* Supreme Court of the United States. Argued December 10, 1986; decided June 19, 1987; http://www.law.umkc .edu/faculty/proj ects/ftrials/conlaw/edwards.html.

23. See Stephen C. Meyer, " 'Teach the Controversy' on Origins," *Cincinnati Enquirer,* March 30, 2002, p. D7.

24. For the lesson plan, see http://science2.marion.ohio-state .edu/ohioscience/L10-H23_Critical_Analysis.pdf.

25. See "Critical Analysis of Evolution—Grade 10," by the Ohio Department of Education. Quoted from the section Ohio Standard Connection, Benchmark H, online at http://science2 .marion.ohio-state.edu/ohioscience/L10–H23_Critical_Analy sis.pdf.

26. Bruce Albert of the National Academy of Sciences wrote the letter to the Ohio Board of Education, February 9, 2004; http:// science2.marion.ohio-state.edu/ohioscience/NAS_Letter.html.

27. "Ohio Academy of Sciences Criticized for Scare Tactics on Evolution," *Discovery Institute News,* February 24, 2004; http:// www.discovery.org/scripts/viewDB/index.php?command=view &id=1849&program=News-CSC&callingPage=discoMainPage.

28. Discovery Institute Press Release, March 9, 2004, http:// www.sciohio.org/letters04.htm.

29. Lawrence Krauss, "State Board Is Failing to Heed Judicious Call for Sound Science," *Columbus Dispatch,* January 30, 2006; http://genesis1.phys.cwru.edu/krauss/dispatched.html.

30. Lawrence M. Krauss, "How to Make Sure Children Are Scientifically Illiterate," *New York Times,* August 15, 2006.

31. Cf. Charles R. Darwin, "Extracts from the letters to the

General Secretary, on the analogy of the structure of some volcanic rocks with that of glaciers," *Proceedings of the Royal Society of Edinburgh* 2 (1845): 17–18; Charles R. Darwin, [Announcement of the award of a Royal Medal to Sir John Richardson], *Proceedings of the Royal Society of London* 8 (1856–57): 257–58.

32. Cf. "Nearly Two-thirds of U.S. Adults Believe Human Beings Were Created by God," The Harris Poll #52, July 6, 2005; http://www.harrisinteractive.com/harris_poll/index.asp?PID=581.

33. See James Glanz, "Science vs. the Bible: Debate Moves to the Cosmos," *New York Times,* October 10, 1999; http://query.nytimes.com/gst/fullpage.html?res=9B0CE4DB1F31F933A257 53C1A96F958260.

34. See Steven Weinberg, "A Designer Universe?" *New York Review of Books,* October 21, 1999. The text was also posted online on August 13, 2004, at http://www.mtsu.edu/rshoward/weinberg.pdf.

35. For information on the discovery, see Jim Baggott, *Perfect Symmetry: The Accidental Discovery of Buckminsterfullerene* (New York: Oxford University Press, 1995).

36. This quote is often attributed to him. My understanding is that he was referring to the possible existence of extraterrestrial intelligence in the galaxy.

37. Georges Lemaître, "Hypothèse de l'atome primitif," *Nature* 128 (1931): 704–6.

38. Cf. Simon Singh, *Big Bang: The Origin of the Universe* (New York: HarperCollins, 2005), 160.

39. Cf. ibid., 361–62.

40. Cf. Lawrence M. Krauss and Richard Dawkins, "Should Science Speak to Faith?" *Scientific American,* June 19, 2007; http://www.sciam.com/article.cfm?id=should-science-speak-to-faith-extended.

41. See especially Richard Dawkins, *The God Delusion* (Boston: Houghton Mifflin, 2006).

42. Lawrence M. Krauss, *Atom: A Single Oxygen Atom's Journey from the Big Bang to Life on Earth . . . and Beyond* (New York: Back Bay Books, 2002).

43. Cf. Walter Isaacson, *Einstein: His Life and Universe* (New York: Simon & Schuster, 2007), 67.

44. For an account of the controversy, see David H. Thomas, *Skull Wars: Kennewick Man, Archaeology, and the Battle for Native American Identity* (New York: Basic Books, 2000). For the larger picture, see Joseph F. Powell, *First Americans: Race, Evolution, and the Origin of Native Americans* (Cambridge: Cambridge University Press, 2005).

45. Moses Maimonides, *A Guide for the Perplexed.*

46. The passage is excerpted from Einstein's diary. See Walter Isaacson, "Einstein and Faith," *Time,* April 5, 2007.

47. Albert Einstein, *The World as I See It* (New York: Citadel, 2001).

ROBERT WUTHNOW, *"No Contradictions Here"*

1. Julia Williams Robinson, "Religion, Science and Our Identity," *New York Times,* October 7, 2005, p. 28.

2. John S. Torday, "Can Science and Religion Co-exist?" *New York Times,* August 24, 2005, p. 16.

3. Manfred Weidhorn, "It's Science or Religion," *New York Times,* October 8, 2005, p. 14.

4. Albert Einstein, "Science, Philosophy and Religion: A Symposium," in *Conference on Science, Philosophy and Religion in Their Relation to the Democratic Way of Life* (New York: Jewish Theological Seminary, 1941); quoted in Gordy Slack, "When Science and Religion Collide or Why Einstein Wasn't an Atheist," *Mother Jones* (November/December 1997); http://www.mother jones.com/news/feature/1997/11/slack.html. Stephen Jay Gould, *Rocks of Ages: Science and Religion in the Fullness of Life* (New York: Ballantine, 1999).

5. Thomas Frank, *What's the Matter with Kansas? How Conservatives Won the Heart of America* (New York: Metropolitan Books, 2004).

6. Embraced as one of the keynote speakers at the American Sociological Association meetings in Philadelphia in August 2004, for example, and at a major conference at New York University.

7. Amy Binder, *Contentious Curricula: Afrocentrism and Creationism in American Public Schools* (Princeton, N.J.: Princeton University Press, 2002).

8. See the essays in this collection by Lawrence Krauss and Kenneth Miller for accounts of the controversy in Dover, Pennsylvania.

9. CBS News Poll, October 23, 2005, available online through LexisNexis Academic.

10. Max Weber, *The Protestant Ethic and the Spirit of Capitalism* (New York: Charles Scribner's Sons, 1958).

11. Joseph Ben-David, *The Scientist's Role in Society: A Comparative Study* (Englewood Cliffs, N.J.: Prentice-Hall, 1971); Bernard Barber, *Science and the Social Order* (New York: Free Press, 1952).

12. Emile Durkheim, *The Division of Labor in Society* (New York: Free Press, 1915).

13. Gili S. Drori, John W. Meyer, Francisco O. Ramirez, and Evan Schofer, *Science in the Modern World Polity: Institutionalization and Globalization* (Stanford, Calif.: Stanford University Press, 2003), 9.

14. Robert Wuthnow, *Meaning and Moral Order: Explorations in Cultural Analysis* (Berkeley: University of California Press, 1987), 279.

15. Don K. Price, *The Scientific Estate* (Cambridge, Mass.: Harvard University Press, 1965), 18.

16. Richard L. Rogers, "The Role of Elites in Setting Agendas for Public Debate: A Historical Case," in *Vocabularies of Public Life: Empirical Essays in Symbolic Structure,* ed. Robert Wuthnow (London: Routledge, 1992), 234–47.

17. Susan E. Myers-Shirk, " 'To Be Fully Human': U.S. Protestant Psychotherapeutic Culture and the Subversion of the Domestic Ideal, 1945–1965," *Journal of Women's History* 12 (Spring 2000): 112–36.

18. Thomas F. Gieryn, "Boundary-Work and the Demarcation of Science from Non-Science: Strains and Interests in Professional Ideologies of Scientists," *American Sociological Review* 48 (December 1983): 781–95; quotation is from p. 781.

19. Olivia Judson, "Evolution Is in the Air," *New York Times*, November 6, 2005, p. 13.

20. Clifford Geertz, *The Interpretation of Cultures* (New York: Basic Books, 1973), 90.

21. Bruno Latour and Steve Woolgar, *Laboratory Life: The Construction of Scientific Facts*, rev. ed. (Princeton, N.J.: Princeton University Press, 1986), 243.

22. Paul Ricoeur, *Freud and Philosophy* (Boston: Beacon, 1970).

23. Richard C. Atkinson, "The Golden Fleece, Science Education, and U.S. Science Policy," *Proceedings of the American Philosophical Society* 143 (September 1999); available at http://works.bepress.com/richard_atkinson/48.

24. Elaine Howard Ecklund and Christopher P. Scheitle, "Religious Differences Between Natural and Social Scientists: Preliminary Results from a Study of 'Religion Among Academic Scientists (RAAS),'" paper presented at the Annual Meetings of the Association for the Sociology of Religion, Philadelphia, August 14, 2005.

25. Penny Edgell, Joseph Gerteis, and Douglas Hartmann, "Atheists as 'Other': Moral Boundaries and Cultural Membership in American Society," *American Sociological Review* 71 (2006): 211–34.

26. Abraham Heschel, "Answer to Einstein," *Conservative Judaism* 55 (Summer 2003): 39–41. I am grateful to Martin Kavka for this source; see his "The Meaning of That Hour: Prophecy, Phenomenology and the Public Sphere in the Early Writings of Abraham Joshua Heschel," in *Religion and the Secular in a Violent World: Politics, Terror, Ruins,* ed. Clayton Crockett (Charlottesville: University of Virginia Press, 2007).

27. Annie Dillard, *For the Time Being* (New York: Knopf, 1999), 30.

28. C. P. Snow, "The Two Cultures," *New Statesman* 52 (October 6, 1956): 413–14.

29. Roger Kimball, "The Two Cultures Today," *The New Criterion* 12 (February 1994).

30. Philip E. Converse, "The Nature of Belief Systems in Mass

Publics," in *Ideology and Discontent*, ed. David Apter (New York: Free Press, 1964).

31. Geertz, *Interpretation of Cultures*, 142–69.

32. Leon Festinger, *A Theory of Cognitive Dissonance* (Evanston, Ill.: Row and Peterson, 1957); for criticisms, see Charles G. Lord, "Was Cognitive Dissonance Theory a Mistake?" *Psychological Inquiry* 3 (1992): 339–42.

33. Robert Wuthnow, *Acts of Compassion: Caring for Others and Helping Ourselves* (Princeton, N.J.: Princeton University Press, 1991).

34. Kenneth J. Gergen, *The Saturated Self: Dilemmas of Identity in Contemporary Life* (New York: Basic Books, 1991), 73–74.

35. *Kitzmiller v. Dover*, 400 F. Supp. 2d 707 (M.D. Pa. 2005), pp. 8–10.

36. Alan Wolfe, *One Nation, After All: What Americans Really Think About God, Country, Family, Racism, Welfare, Immigration, Homosexuality, Work, the Right, the Left, and Each Other* (Baltimore: Penguin, 1999). The words in quotes are mine, not from the book, but based on remarks by Professor Wolfe during a personal conversation.

37. See, for instance, James Davison Hunter, *Culture Wars: The Struggle to Define America* (New York: Basic Books, 1991).

38. On this point, see especially Wilfred M. McClay, review of *One Nation, After All* by Alan Wolfe, *Commentary* 105 (May 1998).

39. Ecklund and Scheitle, "Religious Differences Between Natural and Social Scientists."

40. Robert Wuthnow, *After Heaven: Spirituality in America Since the 1950s* (Berkeley: University of California Press, 1998).

41. Christian Smith, *Soul Searching: The Religious and Spiritual Lives of American Teenagers* (New York: Oxford University Press, 2005), 96.

42. National Science Foundation, *Science and Technology: Public Attitudes and Public Understanding* (Washington, D.C.: Government Printing Office, 2004).

Contributors

HAROLD W. ATTRIDGE

Dean of Yale University Divinity School & Lillian Claus Professor of New Testament

Dean Attridge has made scholarly contributions to New Testament exegesis and to the study of Hellenistic Judaism and the history of the early Church. His publications include *Hebrews: A Commentary on the Epistle to the Hebrews* and *Nag Hammadi Codex I: The Jung Codex*. He has edited numerous books, including *Psalms in Community*, with Margot Fassler. He has been active in the Society of Biblical Literature, which he served as president in 2001.

LAWRENCE M. KRAUSS

Foundation Professor in the School of Earth and Space Exploration and Director of the Origins Initiative at Arizona State University

Lawrence Krauss is a theoretical physicist with wide research interests, including the interface between elementary particle physics and cosmology, where his studies include the early universe, the nature of dark matter, general relativity, and neutrino astrophysics. He is the author of seven best-selling books, including *The Physics of Star Trek*.

KENNETH R. MILLER

Professor of Biology, Brown University

Kenneth R. Miller is a cell biologist whose interests extend to evolutionary theory and the interface between science and religion. He was an expert witness in the 2005 Dover, Pennsylvania, lawsuit challenging a school board mandate to incorporate intelligent design into the curriculum. He is the author of *Finding Darwin's God: A Scientist's Search for the Common Ground Between God and Evolution* and, more recently, of *Only a Theory: Evolution and the Battle for America's Soul.*

RONALD L. NUMBERS

Hilldale Professor of the History of Science and Medicine and of Religious Studies, University of Wisconsin–Madison

Ronald Numbers has written or edited more than two dozen books, including *The Creationists, Darwinism Comes to America,* and *Galileo Goes to Jail and Other Myths about Science and Religion.*

ALVIN PLANTINGA

John A. O'Brien Professor of Philosophy, University of Notre Dame

Alvin Plantinga is a contemporary American philosopher known for his work in epistemology, metaphysics, and the philosophy of religion. His books include *God Freedom and Evil, God and Other Minds: A Study of the Rational Justification of Belief in God, Warranted Christian Belief,* and *Knowledge of God.*

KEITH THOMSON

Professor emeritus of natural history, University of Oxford
Senior research fellow, American Philosophical Society

Keith Thomson is the author of more than two hundred scientific articles and twelve books, including *The Common but Less Frequent Loon and Other Essays,* published by Yale University Press.

ROBERT WUTHNOW

Gerhard R. Andlinger Professor of Sociology and Director of
the Center for the Study of Religion, Princeton University

Robert Wuthnow has conducted pathbreaking research on diverse facets of American religion, including economics, politics, arts, and psychology. His works include *After Heaven: Spirituality in America Since the 1950s* and *After the Baby Boomers: How Twenty and Thirty Somethings Are Reshaping the Future of American Religion.* He is the editor of the *Encyclopedia of Religion and Politics.*

Index